# A Perfect Start

# A Perfect Start

**Or coping with the first months of parenthood**

## Christine and Peter Hill

**Vermilion**
**LONDON**

1 3 5 7 9 10 8 6 4 2

First published as *You and Your New Baby* in 1996 and 1999
by Vermilion

This revised edition published in 2007 by Vermilion, an imprint
of Ebury Publishing

A Random House Group company

The Random House Group Limited Reg. No. 954009

Addresses for companies within the Random House Group can be found at
www.randomhouse.co.uk

A CIP catalogue record for this book is available from the British Library

The Random House Group Limited supports The Forest Stewardship
Council (FSC), the leading international forest certification organisation.
All our titles that are printed on Greenpeace approved FSC certified paper
carry the FSC logo. Our paper procurement policy can be found at
www.rbooks.co.uk/environment

**Mixed Sources**
Product group from well-managed
forests and other controlled sources
www.fsc.org  Cert no. TT-COC-2139
© 1996 Forest Stewardship Council
FSC

Printed in Great Britain by
Clays Ltd, St Ives plc

ISBN 9780091917425

Copies are available at special rates for bulk orders. Contact the sales
development team on 020 7840 8487 for more information.

To buy books by your favourite authors and register for offers, visit
www.rbooks.co.uk

The advice offered in this book is not intended to be a substitute for
the advice and counsel of your personal physician. Neither the authors
nor the publisher can be held responsible for any loss or claim arising
out of the use, or misuse, of the suggestions made, or the failure to
take medical advice.

*To baby Ronnie, whose timely arrival kept us in touch with what we thought we knew*

# CONTENTS

# ACKNOWLEDGEMENTS

In Christine's practice it is routine to de-brief every woman within days of her birth. The purpose of this is to establish how her labour went, whether she has had any problems in the post-natal period and to check that her baby is feeding well. This is repeated a few weeks later to confirm that mother and baby are thriving. We'd like to thank the thousands of women who have shared their experiences with us in this way.

We would also like to thank our colleagues:

Barbara Whiteford, specialist physiotherapist in women's health, especially for help with current thinking about pelvic floor issues and for sharing her experience as a hospital-based physiotherapist.

Clare Byam-Cook, midwife and baby feeding specialist, who has helped hundreds of babies and mothers with feeding problems.

Dr Ian Hay, erstwhile Professor of Paediatrics at Pretoria, South Africa, and now consultant paediatrician at the Portland Hospital for Women and Children, London, for his paediatric wisdom.

We have been very lucky to have Julia Kellaway as our editor. Her support, patience and encouragement during the writing of the manuscript were really helpful.

# First Remarks

This is a book for first-time mothers and fathers, particularly those who are used to running their own lives and have successful jobs or lifestyles. The months after the birth of a first child are wonderful and magical – but also a time when most new parents are very likely to feel surprisingly helpless and useless; something they had never expected. For those who normally consider themselves in charge, such emotions are doubly unsettling. Generally speaking, the older and higher up the career ladder you are, the greater the impact. If you are used to a high-pressure job and can handle crises with aplomb, your precious new baby can expose a vulnerability you did not know you had.

**This is, in many ways, a book for those who think they are not going to need it.**

Its focus is the first few months after a baby's birth, but it is not just about babies; it is also about the adults who look after them, about becoming a parent. Although we mainly address mothers, we obviously hope fathers will want to read as much as possible, and we have kept them in mind throughout.

Some parts are intentionally short. We notice, and indeed remember, that late pregnancy and new mother-hood are not the times for digesting lengthy text.

We have updated our first book, *You and Your New Baby*, because we still haven't found an adequate guide that helps new parents adjust to the process of becoming a parent, something that is a very substantial shift in their own lives. A pregnant woman is the centre of attention until her baby is born. But at the precise moment of birth the baby becomes the focus of everyone's interest – and occupies centre-stage while his mother is displaced to the wings. Much has been written about how to look after babies but little about how new parents can look after themselves and each other. The issue may have been overlooked.

In over 30 years of professional practice we have, between us, been involved with more than five thousand women and their new babies. During this period Christine has run antenatal and postnatal classes for women and has, by now, heard just about every question that women at this stage of their lives can ask. Peter has discussed new parenthood and parenting with many of Christine's patients but, more importantly, has worked as a child psychiatrist with an expert interest in child development, most recently at Great Ormond Street Hospital for Children and now mainly in private practice. Child psychiatrists spend most of their time talking to parents, especially mothers, and always ask about pregnancies, births and the feelings and issues surrounding them. What is striking is that all women say: 'No one can ever prepare you for coming home with your first baby.' We hope we can. That is what this book is all about.

You will notice that we have made the baby male. Nobody has found a way round the problem of how to talk about gender without being unfair or sounding contrived. Calling all babies 'he' makes it easier for the reader when both baby and mother are referred to in the same sentence.

We also assume that babies have two parents who live together and are married. Obviously this is not always true, but the use of the term 'husband' makes writing (and reading) easier by cutting down on all the terms that otherwise could be used to refer to fathers, partners or their equivalent. There is another reason, too. We don't use the term 'your baby's father' all the time because fathers, like mothers, are other things as well.

Most women still have their first baby in hospital (which we think is the safest place for a first birth) and this why there are sections specifically about being in hospital.

However, modern healthcare practice (possibly exacerbated by the current midwife shortage) means that mothers are discharged from hospital much earlier than used to be the case. It is increasingly common for first-time mothers to deliver their baby in the morning (after missing a night's sleep) and find themselves back at home the same afternoon feeling somewhat dazed. In our experience they are not uncommonly frightened as well.

Never before have so many new parents returned home with their baby, hours after the birth, to find themselves on their own with minimal professional support. This book takes you through day by day and then week by week, detailing precisely what to expect and how to cope.

What is striking is how the same issues and problems keep coming up and we have had plenty of opportunity to learn from feedback on how helpful our advice has been. With increasing experience we have found out what is important, what usually works and what doesn't. We'd like to pass this on so that you have a better chance of enjoying your baby and the whole process of becoming a parent. We really want this to be a good time in your life rather than some sort of assault course.

# PART ONE:
## Thinking Ahead

# CHAPTER 1:

## Moving on ...

You want to do the best – for all of you. A perfect start for your baby, for you as a new mother, and for your husband as a new father.

Let's assume you have already done a number of things during your pregnancy:

- Tried to be sensible about diet, smoking, alcohol, etc.
- Made the effort to get some rest during the daytime (even though it has sometimes been difficult to arrange).
- Registered with an antenatal clinic or obstetrician and booked in somewhere for the birth.
- Had a look at a book on pregnancy and birth – at least as far as the sections on complications, which made you feel panicky.
- Bought some nursing bras and baby equipment (see page 36).
- Attended some antenatal classes to ensure you are reasonably well-informed and prepared for the birth. (If not, it is really important to try and book a condensed weekend class at your hospital or through the National Childbirth Trust.)

- Learned how to contract and relax your pelvic floor muscles, and have been doing so.

All this is fairly routine, yet there are a couple of other issues.

One is the fact that your baby's life has already started. He is there, very much alive but inside you. **You have been already looking after him perfectly by looking after yourself.** This is the way to go on when he starts to live *outside* you.

Birth is a milestone in his life, not the start of it. The second issue is therefore not to over-focus on birth – you don't necessarily need to book the birthing pool, download the ideal birth plan or light the candles in order to give him a 'perfect' start since he's already ahead of you. Also, although you need to be well-informed and prepared for the birth, you can't do much to influence how it will go. His birth will be largely dictated by him (the position he is lying in when you go into labour) and by the shape of your pelvis.

We have met so many women who plan a 'perfect' birth but are then subsequently distraught because it didn't go the way they expected. They feel that it was somehow their fault if they needed an assisted delivery or perhaps a Caesarean section, and because of this their baby has got off to a bad start (even though they have a wonderful baby).

In any case, what is a 'perfect' birth? Perfect for whom? The mother, the father, the baby, or the midwife? Some women would describe a perfect birth as an elective Caesarean and some as a drug-free water birth. Both views are valid. **There is no such thing as a 'perfect' birth that is applicable to everyone.**

What has been shown over and over again is that it is the quality of continuing care throughout childhood which counts in human development – not whether the mother had an epidural, for instance. A 'perfect' birth:

- is not in itself sufficient for a perfect start
- isn't required for perfect baby development
- does not guarantee a perfect child.

What really matters is that you and your baby are OK. Don't pin everything on the birth and, for goodness' sake, don't believe you have failed as a woman and mother if it doesn't go the way you wanted.

Your baby's future does not depend upon an absolutely perfect start. There are many starts and stages and a progression as your baby begins his life inside you, then outside you, later gathering independence in some things but not in others. No stage is critical as far as your management of things is concerned. You can make mistakes and they will not be disasters. We want you to experience the early months of your baby after birth as a good time and for your baby to be a source of joy to you and his father. The chances of this happening increase if you are prepared for some of the problems, hassles, joys, stresses, practicalities and possible hurdles that are ahead.

## IT'S NOT GOING TO CHANGE MY LIFE (OR IS IT?)

During pregnancy, babycare happens automatically. Your baby is inside you, and, so long as you look after yourself, he is looked after, too. When you give birth and your baby starts to live outside your body, you are going to have to actively look after him. This means you have to re-organise quite a chunk of your life, especially as new babies require looking after during the night as well as during the day. For most people this is a bit of a shock to the system because they haven't foreseen the magnitude of it. They are ambushed. How come?

When you become a parent for the first time, the world changes. Having a baby is even more of a life change than getting married – the other big commitment you make to share your life permanently with someone you love. There's absolutely no divorce possibility this time. You will fall in love with your baby just as you did with your husband and, like a husband, a baby makes demands on your time. This phrase – 'makes demands on your time' – trips past quickly because it is a cliché, but this is exactly what happens. Babies are very demanding.

This does not just stem from the practicalities of having to look after a baby. Even if you have a full-time nanny, you will find that, because you love him so much, your baby will occupy a staggering amount of your thoughts and emotional energy because you will find yourself constantly thinking and perhaps worrying about him. If he needs you he will cry, something which is impossible to dismiss. You may be able to ignore the crying of other people's babies but not your own. He will make you feel both proud and sometimes helpless. Life honestly won't be as it was before. **Babies make it impossible for their parents to remain the people they used to be.**

What makes something so small, lovely and helpless as a baby so powerful that he will change your life? Partly it is the force of his sheer helplessness. He has to be cared for because it is so obvious that he can't do anything for himself. Babies have a well-developed capacity to elicit good parenting so that they survive; they have to make sure that someone looks after them. They can't exist on their own and won't be able to for another dozen or so years.

Of course, that is not the whole story. A baby has the knack of ensuring that you get hooked on him; he makes you fall in love with him. Before you become pregnant, babies seem quite nice but not absolutely wonderful. Yet when you have your own he will quite simply bowl you over. He will make you want to pick him up, cuddle him, love him, and he will plant roots in your heart and mind for ever. That's another way in which he ensures his own survival. It is also a way of making things enjoyable and fulfilling for you.

There is also something very special about your own baby. He is individual, unique, irreplaceable and terribly precious. It is not just that he has the equipment selected by evolution to ensure his survival by eliciting caring responses from adults; he forms a unique relationship with you. He is not just any old baby; he is yours and you are his. A special relationship develops between the two of you.

For some mothers this is easy. From the moment of birth, or sometimes months beforehand, they are in love with their baby. For quite a number of others, such feelings take some time to grow and there is no instant 'bonding', but a love affair that develops later. **Do not panic that you may be the only woman in the world who will not fall in love with her baby; he will make sure that you do.**

Your baby has an effect on you directly, something that continues throughout his childhood and beyond. It isn't just the case that you will bring him up; he will also bring out aspects of you which might not otherwise have happened. **Parents bring up their children, of course, but children bring up parents, too.** By their very existence they encourage their parents to learn about a whole new universe of child-related topics – toys, schools or childhood illnesses – which most adults would not otherwise bother with. They elicit new emotions from parents, such as pride in their achievements, and they make sure that their parents acquire new skills, whether these be changing nappies or playing undiscovered computer games.

# PLANNING AHEAD

One of the differences between parents who are competent and those who are not is the extent to which competent parents are pro-active. They plan ahead rather than yield passively to a situation which then swamps them.

So why do so few parents-to-be, who are otherwise capable people, take time to do this?

Often there are some magical yet substantial blocks that haunt a surprising number of sensible and stable women in pregnancy:

- A curious barrier which prevents many women believing that they will soon be actually holding their own baby; that the forthcoming baby is just too good to be true and might not happen. (This is why it was difficult to concentrate at the breast-feeding talk at your antenatal class.)
- A feeling of dread that if one buys too many baby clothes and makes too many preparations then the baby will die.
- Oddly conflicting emotions of anticipation, anxiety and mild feelings of gloominess – 'Have I made a frightful mistake? Do I really want all this respon-sibility?' These private thoughts can be triggered simply by the gift of yet another home-knitted acrylic matinée jacket coupled with the words 'Aren't you excited?'
- Getting hung up on a fear of labour and a growing assumption that this is going to be much more of a hurdle than looking after the baby.
- Feeling really fed up with being pregnant and just wanting labour to start.

Yet the most common thought pattern of pregnant women that gets in the way of forward planning is surprisingly banal. It is focusing on labour and birth as the finale, especially if labour is perceived as something which a real woman has to succeed at by having a 'natural' birth. Everything after the birth disappears into small print.

Does it matter? You can, of course, move into the joys of parenthood without giving it that much thought – after all, most people do. Indeed, they may not want to think about what it entails at all. Better not to think about all that, they say. Things will work out. Everyone copes in the end. Let's just enjoy it.

But sometimes they don't cope that well and become demoralised and exhausted (and don't enjoy it). Certainly you will survive if you don't think ahead, but at a cost to yourself and your marriage. It isn't simply a question of driving yourself hard and muddling through. Does your baby really want you to be exhausted, irritable and feeling useless? Does he want to hear you and your husband snapping at each other? While everyone with a young baby gets tired and stressed at some point, it can be cut to a minimum.

By making a small number of arrangements, you are less likely to be knocked sideways by the changes in your life. Even so, many (probably most) women will find themselves thrown off balance. Thinking things through beforehand will enable you to regain your equilibrium sooner, keep your confidence and thus manage better. Most importantly, you are then much more likely to enjoy it all.

Any career woman with spirit will probably say that surely, like any other challenge, a new baby can be managed without having to adjust too much. Surely one can go straight back to work, pick up just where one left off, text the nanny a series of instructions, dispatch the baby to a day nursery by courier, arrange to be contacted if it's time for a feed, and so forth. Quite right in some respects – motherhood shouldn't take over the whole of a woman's life – but in order for the mother to enjoy her baby and continue to enjoy her work, some adjustments to her own life – and that of her husband – are necessary.

# CHAPTER 2:

## The myth of the perfect start

Of course, you will be anxious to get things absolutely right and give your baby the best possible start in life. A perfect start, in fact.

But minor complications may have resulted in your carefully constructed birth plan being thrown out of the window – and you then feel you have failed irrevocably. You might have had the birth experience you wanted, but, inevitably, some of you won't! If you are one of the latter, then you may have spent precious time since your baby has been born looking back at your labour feeling disappointed, rather than enjoying your baby.

No amount of antenatal exercise, diet and yoga can guarantee that your labour follows the path you want. As previously mentioned, the baby's position and the shape of your pelvis will determine how he is born. Although most babies do manage to have a perfectly normal birth, some get stuck, their placenta misbehaves or they get into difficulties so that the labour has to be actively managed. If this happens, it is not likely to be the fault of your obstetrician or midwife. It certainly won't be your fault, either. It really is not a disaster if you found that you unexpectedly needed an epidural or had to have a

Caesarean section. Thank goodness for Caesareans; they save lives.

If one takes the baby's viewpoint, it has to be said that a perfect start for him is absolutely not dependent on a 'natural' birth – be it a water birth, hypno-birth, or whatever. He will not care and none of these will be of much use to him. He won't protest about a ventouse or forceps if they mean he (and you) survive. Let's be quite clear: **a perfect birth is one that results in a healthy baby and mother, no more than that.**

Babies are remarkably birth-proof. Nature does not depend upon things going perfectly, and budgets for minor complications. Babies simply don't need every detail to be absolutely perfect. They really, really don't.

Nor are very early life circumstances (such as what happens in the first few weeks and months) overwhelmingly important for your baby's future development and personality. It is a common fallacy to think that the earlier an influence on a child, the more powerful it will be. If you fire an arrow at a target, a small difference in your aim means a huge difference in where the arrow eventually ends up. The temptation is to think that children are like this – give them an ideal start and they will develop ideally; get it slightly wrong at the start and disaster will follow later in life. But the development of children is just not like that. It depends on continuing processes rather than events. **An early event in itself is not likely to be important unless it persists and turns from an event into something that lasts.** Missing a meal is not important but continually being starved would be.

Obviously, we have to exclude devastating physical illnesses or injuries from this, but many less serious physical problems, which seem alarming at the time, can have their effects diluted by what is called 'good-enough' parenting (see page 235) throughout the childhood years.

In one study, significant birth complications (mainly lack of oxygen) meant that affected babies were behind in their development at one year of age. But in good-quality homes these babies were normal by the age of 10. Sadly, in very poor-quality homes with poverty, parental strife and some neglect, the development of similar babies fell further behind normal in the same period. What mattered was what went on over time, not what happened at birth.

So do not be seduced by the myth of the perfect start as far as birth is concerned. It may be a nice thing to aim for but it is certainly not crucial for your baby.

Nor are bad experiences early in life a big deal. Every mother remembers something dreadful which she allowed to happen to her baby – letting him fall out of his Moses basket, or realising too late that he had been crying with hunger for several days when she thought he was having enough food. She may have a haunting fear that the baby will remember the incident all his life and blame her. Actually, it is virtually unknown for anyone to remember anything from their first two years of life, and most people's earliest memory is at about three-and-a-half years of age. Even after that, memories are extremely fragmentary.

With that in mind, don't get carried away with the idea that birth can be psychologically traumatic for a baby. There was a fashion some years ago for trying to minimise the 'stress' of transferring from a peaceful womb to a bright and noisy outside world by measures such as giving birth in the dark, under water, and to the strains of Mozart, but the generation born with such attention doesn't seem to be any more serene and well-adjusted, or less likely to binge-drink.

Many people assume that babies are passive and therefore it is up to their parents to get everything right for them. But, as we have pointed out elsewhere, babies take an active part in their own development. Right from the start they establish a relationship with you and they carry on developing within a setting of human relationships in which they are active participants. They are not like plants which require merely that you provide water, light and potting compost for their growth. It means that there continue to be many opportunities for things to correct themselves, even if they appear to have gone wrong. Hang on to the idea that, in development, nothing is for ever.

# BONDING

There is another piece of thinking that may worry you unnecessarily. About 30 years ago (perhaps when your parents were giving birth to you) some paediatricians became convinced, on the basis of a few small studies, that the first few days of a baby's life were crucial in establishing an emotional bond between mother and child.

In particular, it was said, a mother had to have skin-to-skin contact with her baby for several hours a day. If this was prevented by physical separation she would never achieve truly loving feelings towards him, there would be a failure of 'bonding' and the baby's development would be slowed in some areas.

Frankly, this is nonsense. The early studies were contradicted by later ones and some myths should now be laid to rest.

For instance, skin-to-skin contact is not absolutely necessary. Being able to handle and cuddle your own baby in his first few days helps you to love him but it is not an all-or-nothing principle and doesn't have to include touching his skin a lot. Nevertheless, the number of doctors and midwives who say skin-to-skin contact is crucial (yet haven't read all the scientific literature) is astonishing. Under no circumstances believe someone who says that you will not bond with your baby because you haven't had skin-to-skin contact with him in the hours after birth. (If this were the case, women who had Caesareans under a general anaesthetic would not bond – and they patently do. For goodness' sake!)

Rather similarly, modern midwifery practice is to vigorously encourage prolonged skin-to-skin contact between a mother and her new baby as soon as possible after birth to encourage breast-feeding. The effect is small and the practice is not welcomed by many women. Yet the belief that it is crucially important has acquired an almost religious authority and even appears in official recommendations.

Delivering the baby on to your bare tummy for the sole purpose of promoting 'bonding' is nonsense (though if he has a short cord it may be a good place to put him briefly, so long as he doesn't slip off). Allowing a mother and baby to get to know each other face-to-face, clothed or unclothed, after birth is much more to the point. If a baby is held in his mother's arms, her face is just the right distance away from him to bring it into focus for his eyes. Newborn babies are usually alert, actively looking around and particularly responsive to their mother's face. Very bright lights will cause a baby to screw up his eyes, so sensitive staff will dim the lights at this point. Wanting to pick your baby up and hold him in your arms is a natural thing to do. If you want your baby on your tummy, all well and good. But don't imagine that it will, on its own, be the only way of sealing a lasting emotional link between the two of you.

Occasionally, a quite normal new mother doesn't experience spontaneous feelings of love towards her baby at the time of his birth. There are a number of reasons for this: she may be exhausted; she may be frightened that her baby will die and so she withholds her feelings; the baby might be premature or not look like the baby she was expecting; or she may lack self-confidence and feel that she will not be able to care for the baby.

This hardly ever matters in the long run. If you don't feel immediate feelings of love for your baby you will discover these feelings developing within a few days or weeks. It sometimes takes time to fall in love with your baby. Human relationships are not so mechanical that they can be switched on and off by a single event.

A baby quickly learns to recognise his mother, but his love for her develops and strengthens over months, not hours or days. As far as a child's later development is concerned, there are no inevitable long-term consequences simply from so-called 'bonding failure' in the first few days of life.

One of the difficulties for mothers who want to understand these issues is that the whole idea of early 'bonding' has become confused by some professionals with a different process that first starts a few months later, when the baby begins to cling to a particular person, usually his mother, and cries if she leaves him. This develops into a close emotional relationship over a period of months and certainly is a powerful influence on the baby's emotional development. Confusingly, this very different process, which has nothing to do with the mother's feelings just after birth, is sometimes called 'affectional bonding', though 'attachment' is a more usual term. It is led by the baby and has proportionally more to do with the baby's emotions than the mother's. To make the muddle worse, the term 'attachment' is now some-times being used to include a mother's love for her newborn baby, which is really confusing.

Nevertheless, the message for you is straightforward: don't panic. You may or may not fall in love with your baby immediately. It doesn't matter. If you are worried that you won't, then the paradox is that you are the sort of person who will become a caring, loving parent. You need not feel that you have to go along with someone else's ideas about the proper thing to do with your newborn baby if it feels silly or wrong – and you don't have to feel guilty or apprehensive that you will disturb some magical process.

# CHAPTER 3:

## Thinking ahead about yourself as a new mother

A new baby is wonderful: you will love him and indeed he will love you. He will provide you with one of the closest and most rewarding relationships you will ever experience and, as he grows and develops, your sense of excitement and achievement will be extraordinary.

As well as the good news, there are some tricky bits, which you will manage better if you anticipate them. You may well find yourself simultaneously exhilarated and exhausted (sleep-deprived) during the first few weeks.

Your world will centre around caring for your baby, so the fun things you do now (such as going out with friends) will be more difficult to arrange. You will fall into step with your baby's demands and routines, and find it impossible to ignore his calls on your time. Having spent much of the pregnancy secretly worrying as to whether their babies will be all right, many women find it hard to relax, even when they have a perfect baby. They continue to nurture another secret worry as to whether their baby will remain all right. This leads to emotional fatigue on top of physical tiredness.

As an extension of this, you will not exactly have time on your hands. Looking after a new baby is very much a full-time job. Your timetable will not allow you many opportunities for shopping, cooking, entertaining or, indeed, resting when you feel like it. In fact, you should expect to be in or around your bed for the first week when you come home from hospital.

Your emotional life will change. Most women find that in the first few weeks after childbirth they are more emotionally volatile and dependent upon their husband and others than before. They cry and fret more readily than they usually do. This is especially marked during the 'baby blues' phase a few days after birth (see page 98) though it frequently persists at a lower degree of intensity for several weeks after returning home. It is almost certainly caused by hormonal changes interacting with the extraordinary experience of birth and a new baby. This emotional turbulence is likely to be coupled with a surprising difficulty in making unimportant decisions and following simple instructions. All this can come as a bit of a shock to competent, organised women (and to their husbands).

At the same time, it is a very common experience for new mothers to find themselves worrying about all sorts of minor things to do with their babies, something which can make them feel that they have lost their sense of proportion and judgement. This contributes to a crisis of confidence which occurs in just about everyone – including new mothers who happen to be paediatricians!

What this means is that, once you come home after the birth, you are going to need some practical and emotional support. **This is especially vital if you are likely to be discharged from hospital within 24 hours of**

**giving birth.** If someone else is helpin[g]
practicalities and minor hassles as well a[s]
confidence (should it start to flag) the[n]
more time for the positive aspects of looking after a new
baby.

# YOUR HUSBAND

He should try to plan his work schedule so that he is
available to be with you, not just when you are in labour
but when you come home, too. Planning for this is not
quite as easy as it might seem, as 'expected date of delivery'
(EDD) is an informed guess rather than a certainty. It is not
uncommon for babies to be born two weeks either side of
their EDD, and although there isn't much point in your
husband taking time off work if you are in hospital, he will
need to be free in the early evening to visit you.

Incidentally, if he is planning to take *statutory* paternity leave (one or two weeks) he needs to apply to his
employer 15 weeks in advance.

Indeed, if you are in hospital for a couple of days
following a Caesarean section you will also be dependent upon him to do any shopping you might need
(mainly food), and possibly to wash and return your
nightdresses.

Because you are used to coping well at home, you might
be tempted to tell him that he shouldn't worry about taking
time off and that you will be able to manage without him if
his work can't be shifted. Although this is generous and
understanding of you, it is one of those things that will
increase the stress on you, thus making it more difficult to
enjoy your baby. In any case (believe it or not), you will
want to see your husband as often as possible.

# ORGANISING SUPPORT FOR THE FIRST FEW DAYS

The obvious person to give you a hand when you come out of hospital is your husband. In practice, his work may not allow enough time off to support you, so you will need further back-up. Contrary to what you might think, your mother is usually the best bet – and she does at least love you. If your mother is not available, the next best thing may be your mother-in-law. Failing this, perhaps another member of your family might be prepared to give a hand – an aunt or sister or sister-in-law.

## Mothers and mothers-in-law

You will need a preliminary discussion with your husband as to whether you should ask your mother (or his) to stay at some point when you come home (if you have the space). But many mothers will have as demanding and pressurised a job as you have and simply won't be able to drop everything without several weeks' warning. Obviously, you need to be careful not to assume that either of your mothers spends all her time dead-heading the roses and waiting for you to ring, so it's best to think ahead and check their availability and willingness.

If one of them is able and willing to help you, *and* you would like her help, as a general rule it is better to stagger the support.

All this means that, if possible, the two of you could plan for your husband to take two or three days off work when you come home. After that, your mother or his might come to stay when he has gone back to work. It is difficult for everyone to balance things if you, the baby, your husband and your mother are all trying to establish yourselves at home at the same time.

Three generations coming simultaneously into a home where there has previously been one generation can be overwhelming. You, your baby and your husband may need to enjoy the first couple of days on your own as a new family. It seems sensible to capitalise on the fact that this is actually a very good time.

## What on earth is a maternity nurse?

A maternity (or monthly) nurse is someone who is employed to look after a mother and her new baby when they return from hospital. They generally live in your house with you. Conventionally they are engaged for the first four weeks, which is why they are sometimes called monthly nurses. Actually, most families find three weeks is ample.

Their training is varied: some will be midwives or nurses by profession; others may have been trained as a nanny or nursery nurse. Occasionally they have no formal training, but have clocked up a great deal of experience through years of looking after hundreds of new babies.

Maternity nurses are extremely expensive – depending on their experience and qualifications, they charge between £500 and £800 per week (probably more than your mortgage) – and you provide their food and board. This means that only a handful of people are able even to think about having one. Sometimes they are paid for by grandparents.

The case for employing a maternity nurse may be strong if you are expecting twins, if neither of you have available parents or family to hand and/or if you are planning to return to work fairly quickly. If this is the case, your best bet is to ring up agencies that specialise in maternity nurses and nannies. Agencies will charge a fee, but at least they will have drawn up a contract and checked qualifications and references.

Should you be thinking of employing a maternity nurse to help you look after your baby, she will ideally start two or three days after you come home, but this is obviously difficult to arrange with precision. If she starts as soon as you return home, there is still a clear role for your husband, which is looking after *you*. You will need to interview and book a maternity nurse well beforehand, of course.

# FOOD

A trip to the supermarket accompanied by a tiny baby can be very anxiety-provoking and needs to be avoided for as long as possible, so bear in mind that you will be dependent on Internet shopping for at least a couple of weeks.

You won't have the time or the energy for real cooking, but you will want (and need) to eat properly – two good meals a day. This is when siege mentality comes in handy – stock up your larder beforehand with tins of tuna, baked beans and anything nutritious that is easily stored. Fill your freezer with as much frozen fish and homemade goodies – such as pasta sauce, shepherd's pie, casseroles, etc. – that it will hold. You will crave 'real' food rather than instants.

# ORGANISING EVENTS AROUND THE BIRTH PERIOD

It's best to keep your diary blank as far as grand social occasions go, and don't succumb to invitations a long way from home without thinking how you will get back to the hospital if your waters break. In fact, after 37 weeks, most women instinctively feel more comfortable near home.

Remember that if you give a precise due date to your family and friends, they will deluge you with phone calls on that day and every day after it. For some reason this is incredibly irritating, and if your baby is late you will find yourself repeatedly and irrationally apologising for the fact. It is sometimes helpful to change the message on your phones: 'Thank you for calling. No, the baby hasn't arrived yet!'

Your EDD may come and go (and nearly half of all first babies are late), leaving you facing a period of emptiness and anticipation while hanging around waiting for labour to start. This could last two weeks and you may feel you are living in a void. You can avoid the worst of this by actively planning some social activities such as going to the cinema or having supper with friends who won't mind if you have to cancel at the last moment.

**Under no circumstances plan a drinks party at home to celebrate the birth.**

# WHAT TO PACK FOR HOSPITAL

You will need to buy some maternity bras – three if you are planning to breast-feed, and at least one even if you are planning to put your baby directly onto the bottle. It is important that you are fitted by someone who is specifically trained to fit nursing bras. She will know how much extra cup size to allow for when your milk comes through, as well as ensuring you have enough hooks to be able to tighten the bra when your rib cage returns to its original size. The ideal time to be fitted is when you are between 34 and 37 weeks pregnant.

Think about packing a labour bag and a case for your stay in hospital. Hospitals have very little space for personal belongings, so it's better to have a small bag for labour, and another holdall for an overnight stay. Although you might not anticipate staying overnight, an unexpected Caesarean section or an afternoon/evening birth will necessitate it. You can then leave the overnight bag in the car until you know you need it and just bring your labour bag into the hospital. Incidentally, do not go into hospital wearing precious rings or earrings – you cannot go to theatre wearing jewellery with stones, and there are no facilities for storing them apart from your husband's pocket. (And you know what that means.) Make sure you have some cash handy around your EDD for a possible emergency taxi or the hospital car park.

## Labour bag

- your hospital notes (if you have them)
- a nightdress for early labour and afterwards
- lightweight dressing gown and slippers or flip flops
- spongebag – with toothbrush, flannel, towel, etc., and a scrunchie to tie back long hair
- if you have contact lenses, take the case and some glasses in case you find the lenses uncomfortable during labour
- a watch with a second hand, to time contractions
- portable music source and a magazine (if you have an epidural, you may have several hours to fill)
- a pair of disposable or old pants, and a couple of maternity pads for after delivery
- nappy, vest and swaddling sheet
- camera (to take photos of your baby, rather than the birth)
- snacks for you (and your husband) after delivery
- anything else suggested by your antenatal class tutor.

## Overnight holdall

This list obviously depends on your anticipated length of stay and what your hospital provides.

For you:
- two extra nightdresses and extra pants
- nursing bra
- more snack food – e.g., dried fruit, fruit juice and chocolate
- notepad and pen – you may well feel fairly brain-dead and need to write down the time you last fed your baby
- tissues/loo paper
- carrier bag for dirty laundry
- two small (coloured) towels – white ones are more likely to be swept up into hospital laundry
- your own pillow – with a coloured pillowcase.

For your baby:
- extra baby clothes if not provided by the hospital
- disposable nappies and muslins (to mop up sick)
- baby soap or aqueous cream and large cotton wool balls to wash his bottom
- bottle, teat and a carton of first infant milk in case of a feeding emergency.

## Car seat

Try to have this ready at home by the time you are 37 weeks pregnant, as you will need it in order to bring your baby home. It is compulsory for babies travelling in a car to be strapped into a separate car seat, and most of these are rear-facing. If your car has an airbag, the car seat cannot be fitted on the front seat. Buying it well in advance of your EDD will give your husband time to check that it actually fits into your particular car (believe it or not, not all seats fit all types of cars) and to work out where the straps go. (This is not a sexist suggestion – you may not be able to stand for very long when you leave hospital so it is likely that it will be your husband, not you, who will be responsible for getting both the car seat and your baby safely strapped in.)

Before going into hospital, put some baby clothes (including a hat) into the car seat for the baby to travel home in. Then, when your husband leaves home to collect you both from hospital, all he has to do is pick up the seat.

## YOUR OTHER (STEP-) CHILDREN

Although this is a book aimed at first-time mothers, some of you will already be mothers, or step-mothers with small children at home. You will obviously have told your child or children that they are going to have a new baby brother or sister. It is surprisingly common for women to worry unreasonably about the impact the new baby might have on an elder child's psyche. Some women even worry that they will not have enough love to go round to include the baby they are carrying. Usually things go smoothly, but you can start to act positively now to minimise any possible difficulties later:

- Tell them what is going to happen: that you will go into hospital (if you do), who will look after them during that time, and that **you will come back** with the new baby.
- Let them feel the bump and the baby's kicks if they want to.
- Allow older children to attend a late scan if you have one. This enables them to 'see' the baby, which

is an easy way of helping them grasp the reality of the situation.

- Involve them as much as possible in the buying of baby equipment or clothes.
- Get them accustomed to the routine of a rest or quiet period in their room after lunch. **This is essential**. You are going to (desperately!) need this time, either to sleep yourself or at least to feed your baby in peace.
- Get them used to spending time with their father and away from your side.
- Buy them a present that the new baby can give them. It must be something that they will find exciting, rather than a stocking present. It also must be wanted. (This almost certainly means not educational!)

Problems with older children's jealousy of the new baby, or their regression to immature or clinging behaviour, are more likely to be a reaction to a change in *your* behaviour – such as being preoccupied with the baby and having less time for them – than the fact of the baby's existence.

Although children can be understandably jealous of the way in which the new baby has taken pride of place in your affections, it has been shown that when a new baby enters the family, most mothers communicate rather more sharply and are more impatient with their older children. Typically, and understandably, they spend less time playing with them. The children sense this and resent it – not unreasonably – and they may or may not take it out on the baby. This is often not so much jealousy of the baby as puzzled anger at the change in you and an inspired guess as to who might be to blame for that.

If you are aware that a new baby might change your attitude and behaviour in such a way, it should (in theory) be easier for you to catch yourself doing it and balance things accordingly. It may be possible, for instance, for your husband or mother to cover babycare for half an hour each day so you can spend some quality time with the older one(s).

# CHAPTER 4:

## Thinking ahead about your baby

This is more than daydreaming about how things will be; it means making preparations, as mentioned in Chapter 1 (see page 7). One important principle is that you should be prepared to be flexible and consider your various options without committing yourself completely until your baby has been born. Baby books can give a very daunting impression of life with a baby; there are often pages and pages of advice on equipment, routines and procedures.

There are a few things you simply must have in stock (nappies, vests and swaddling sheets) and it makes sense to buy them beforehand, but you don't need to get absolutely everything. You cannot always predict what you may be given as presents, either. Friends and family are usually incredibly generous when it comes to buying baby clothes, and many new mothers find they have more first size babygros than their baby can possibly wear. (They then give them to their girlfriends and the cycle continues.) Although, as we have said, it is a good idea to lay in a large stash of food before the birth, the best policy for buying equipment and clothes is to get only the minimum beforehand.

Although your opportunities for shopping will be curtailed in the first few weeks, life goes on after child-birth and you can still buy or borrow what you need when you need it.

Family and friends are usually willing to do something practical to help when you come home with your baby.

# BABY GEAR AND EQUIPMENT

Of course, you will have started to get some baby gear together. Keep a few principles in mind:

- You probably don't need as much as you think.
- Keep all receipts in case you need to change things because your baby arrives bigger or smaller or a different sex than you imagined.
- A 9lb (4kg) baby is considerably larger than a 6lb (2.75kg) baby, and will bypass the first size in vests and sleepsuits.
- You may not know if you prefer sleepsuits or nighties until you actually have your baby.
- Everything has to be stored somewhere.

## Small items

- v-shaped pillow or three extra pillows for feeding
- side light with very low wattage (e.g. 8 watts) bulb for your/baby's bedside (for night feeds, dropped dummies etc., not as a night-light)
- heater with thermostatic control for winter babies
- plug-in baby alarm (you may not actually need this)
- nappies

- nappy bags
- pack of muslin squares (best material for mopping up during and after feeds)
- two changing mats (one upstairs and one downstairs)
- barrier cream for baby's bottom, e.g. zinc and castor oil cream or Sudocrem
- portable changing bag for trips out
- cotton wool balls and wipes
- baby bath solution/non-allergenic baby soap, e.g Simple soap/aqueous cream
- baby bathing sponge
- hairbrush and baby nail scissors/emery boards
- three swaddling sheets (see page 91)
- three sheets for crib/Moses basket and pushchair/ pram
- two blankets for crib/Moses basket and pushchair – wool and cotton cellular
- two soft towels for the baby's use only
- four to six short-sleeved cotton vests (over-the-head type are easier than front ties, and some mothers like those with poppers between the baby's legs)
- four to six nighties or babygros
- cardigans
- socks and hat
- bibs with waterproof back
- bottles and sterilising equipment (even if you plan to breast-feed you may still have to give water/ formula).

Incidentally, contrary to what used to be said, you don't actually need to wash everything before you use it. The exception is new towels, which tend not to dry properly until they have been washed.

*t*

...rge and rapidly changing market with a
pote... bewildering array to choose from. You might
find it best to seek expert advice, not just the view of a
sales assistant in a particular shop. Good examples of
some items may be hard to find (bouncing cradles, for
example), and discovering exactly which high-tech
pushchair is just right for you is not at all straightforward. We have found that Babylist (www.baby
list.co.uk) gives informed advice and stocks a good range.

- *Changing table*
  This is a unit with a flat top surface for the changing
  mat and shelves and drawers below. The top should
  be at the same level as the mother's waist, to prevent
  low backache. Unfortunately, some are far too low,
  especially if unnecessary castors have to be
  removed. A chest of drawers or a small table with a
  shelf below will do just as well – finding something
  the correct height is far more important than
  whether or not it has specific nooks and crannies for
  cotton wool balls.

- *Bouncing cradle*
  Valuable equipment if you can find a good one.
  These allow a baby to sit or lie at various angles
  and are comfortable for the baby (whereas car
  seats, typically, are not). When propped up he can
  see what is going on and where you are. Even very
  small babies can be wrapped up and put in one,
  lying flat so they can be rocked to sleep. Self-
  powered rocking versions (in spite of claims) are
  not always better.

- *Baby bath*

Some mothers use their adult bath right from the start. A baby bath is fairly bulky and, as you won't be using it for more than a few months, borrow from a friend if the offer arises. Otherwise, try to find one that hooks over the sides of your own bath, as this will bring your baby up to a better height (back care again). Some adult baths are fitted too close to the wall to allow the baby bath to sit on it safely – you might want to check this beforehand.

- *Slings*

The principle of a sling is a good one (especially if you have a baby with colic) but it is surprisingly difficult to find a really satisfactory sling that suits both baby and mother (fathers generally need them later). A good sling should contain the baby and steady his head so you can get on with things requiring two hands. You wear it on your front so that you can talk to your baby. Only when he has developed proper head control (at about five to six months) will you be able to put him in a backpack, a different thing altogether and much more suitable for fathers and walks outside.

The sling must be the right height – if it is too low, the weight of your baby will make your lower back arch in just the same way pregnancy does, and therefore give you low backache. The best test for height is whether you can easily kiss your baby's head. Look for adjustable shoulder straps or other ways of adjusting the height (some models have complex backs that perform the same function).

Slings are not essential. Some manufacturers claim that carrying your baby in a sling does wonders for your mutual relationship. There is just a little evidence to support this but the effect is small and only applies to a minority of babies. It is certainly not worth buying an inferior sling and giving yourself a strained back in the cause of furthering your relationship with your baby if the consequence is that it is too painful to pick him up at other times.

- *Moses basket* JTK JIA ·
Not so much a rival to the detachable car seat as something to have in addition. In it, your baby can sleep lying flat while you move him from room to room. Many babies sleep in their basket at night for the first few weeks.

- *Pushchair/pram*
The choice and available technology are awesome. No one model is clearly superior and the features that appeal to one woman (or man) may irritate another. Considerations such as the amount of space in your hall, whether there are steps and stairs to your front door, and whether the pushchair handle comes up to your waist (as it should) are obviously critical. It is best if both of you get expert advice from specialist shops/ departments (or Babylist, see page 38) where you can also have the opportunity to try out different types.

- *Cot*
Although most people start off with their baby in a Moses basket, pushchair top or crib at night, it is

usual to transfer babies to a cot at about three months. It is worth investing in as sturdy (and thus expensive) a model as possible, as it will double up as an early-morning playpen. Toddlers tend to abuse cots by jumping up and down and vigorously rattling the bars, so you will want to check stability and that the drop-side mechanism works impeccably. They will also use the top rail as a teething bar. For these reasons, second-hand cots are not the bargain they might seem.

- *Nursing chair*
  Or other low armless chair with a straight back that is suitable for feeding.

- *Car seat*
  Buy well beforehand (see page 31).

## WHERE IS THE BABY GOING TO SLEEP?

There is no shortage of advice on this point, some of it forcefully expressed. Official guidelines from the Department of Health state that the safest place for your baby to sleep at night for his first six months is in your bedroom but not in your bed.

On the other hand this may not be possible (because your bedroom is too small or the only space available is next to a radiator), and you may fret that this condemns your baby to imminent death. It doesn't. Some, but not all, studies find an association between cot death (which is rare) and sleeping in a different room, but no one knows exactly why and it is probably a reflection of something else and not a cause in its own right. It isn't likely to be because a parent can hear their baby in distress and rescue him, as cot death is silent. Guidelines have to be ultra-cautious by their very nature and simply cannot always be slavishly followed. (See page 230 for more about cot death.)

Rather similarly, you may simply not be able to sleep soundly in the same room as your baby because of his snuffling or the fact that you and he need a different room temperature. To us it seems that he should sleep in whichever place you feel most comfortable with.

As it happens, most couples do indeed start by having their baby sleep in their bedroom in a Moses basket, crib or pushchair top. At what stage he might transfer to his own room is debatable. Cot death prevention literature says not until six months (because cot death is usually before then) but, in practice, most parents we have known move their baby into his own room at about four months.

Consider the various options as they apply to your home, but don't make a final decision until you come out of hospital. What seems a good idea beforehand may not feel right to you later.

Some people consider having their baby in bed with them right from the start. There's plenty of advice against this on safety grounds, and you may be given a leaflet about it. On the other hand, a few ideologists advocate co-sleeping, but there are no emotional advantages for him and a few difficulties. There is a chance that he may overheat under a duvet, which is potentially dangerous. There is a definite increase in the risk of cot death if you are a smoker. Your bed is unlikely to be big enough for three. That usually means that your husband moves out. Indeed, some women capitalise on this as the months wear on and use the baby in bed as a contraceptive.

If you have a big bed and it seems to be the right place for your baby to sleep, yet you are worried that you or your husband will roll over onto him (which is possible, but very unlikely), you can wall off a space with a pillow, and also make sure that neither you nor your husband is drunk or out cold with a sleeping pill. On the other hand, if you are going to wall off a space, your baby might as well be next to your bed but in his own basket or crib.

You may also find out later on that you are the type of mother who sleeps less well when your baby is in your bed. It is very common indeed for women to wake in the night in a confused panic as to whether their babies are or are not in the bed with them, and have or have not suffocated.

You can sense that we have reservations about having your baby always in your bed, though, of course, every parent takes their baby into their bed to sleep from time to time, and may well doze off after a feed before being able to return him to his own bed.

From the baby's point of view, there is no one place that is psychologically more advantageous than any other.

## Blackout blinds?

These are sometimes recommended for your baby's room, presumably so he learns that when it is pitch-black he is supposed to be asleep. Although babies need to have indications of whether it is night or day, we don't think you need blackout blinds for the following reasons:

- They are another expensive hassle.
- Babies need to learn to sleep in the daytime without having to be in a very dark room.
- When you go to stay with your parents and friends, they are unlikely to have them.

# DECISIONS ABOUT FEEDING

The decision to breast- or bottle-feed is like other aspects of babycare. You don't necessarily have to make a firm decision before you have your baby. There will be time afterwards and what you eventually choose must feel right for you both. Some mothers will breast-feed one of their children but not the other, not so much on account of their increasing experience but because the individual personalities of their babies means that it feels right to give one a bottle, the other the breast.

One way of thinking about the decision is not to see it as a stark choice between breast and bottle but a question as to when you will transfer from breast to bottle. Before your milk comes through, the breast produces a yellowish fluid (colostrum) which is rich in protein and, importantly, antibodies against infection. **There are therefore substantial advantages in putting your baby to the breast for the first few days to ensure he gets the goodies from the colostrum, for which no substitute exists.**

You can transfer to a bottle at any time thereafter. In fact (and in spite of what you may be told) you can give both formula and breast milk to your baby if that is what feels right for you. But interestingly enough, some women who are sure they are not going to be able to face breast-feeding are persuaded to give their baby colostrum, and then go on to find the whole breast-feeding thing perfectly all right. Our recommendation is to start by giving breast-feeding a go and make up your mind later.

Breast milk has nutritional advantages over formula milk, as well as one or two other benefits, such as providing better protection against infection and, possibly, against allergies, too. It has had, after all, more than a million years of development. Once established, breast-feeding is easier in the long term as there is absolutely no preparation involved. When all goes well, most mothers find it incredibly rewarding. All authorities agree it is the preferred method for most babies.

However, it has to be said that breast-feeding is initially more difficult and takes longer to establish than formula-feeding. One of the snags associated with breast-feeding is that, if it does prove tricky in the early weeks, there are too many experts with different advice. They usually have very definite views indeed, so that you can easily get confused as a result. The ultimate advice on the subject is a book by Clare Byam-Cook, *What to Expect When You're Breast-feeding ... and What if You Can't?*.

Although breast-feeding is preferable it is certainly not imperative and your baby will thrive perfectly well on a bottle. Formula milk is most definitely adequate for a baby's nutrition. In the long term, it doesn't much matter which approach to opt for. You can't, for instance, tell which university students were breast-fed as babies. Formula-feeding enables your husband and others to help with feeds, especially at night, and gives you more freedom during the day. Being technically much easier to establish it goes more smoothly in the early weeks. It is seductive because you can see how much milk is going in! If you know you will be formula-feeding right from the start, you may need to be quite assertive and clear about this so that you can get the appropriate professional advice.

Even if you know you are going to breast-feed, it is highly likely that you will want to give your baby a bottle of expressed breast milk at some stage, so you might as well buy the equipment before the birth. You then have time to practise all the rituals of cleaning, sterilising and warming in case you have to do it for real in the presence of an urgently screaming, hungry baby.

However you are going to feed, make sure you have a decent chair to sit in while you are doing so. This means an old-fashioned nursing chair if you can find one. Otherwise use a low-seated, high-backed, armless chair of the sort often found in bedrooms. You will probably need to buy extra pillows: three to lean against when you are feeding in bed; one for the baby, who may need to lie placed on your lap (to bring him up to your breast); and possibly another under your thighs to take your weight off painful stitches.

# NAMES

Unless you are quite sure of the sex of your future baby (and ultrasound is not completely reliable on this score, though amniocentesis is), be very careful not to get too hung up on the idea that you are going to have a baby of one particular sex. It is remarkably easy to become convinced you are going to have a girl, so that you choose only girls' names. You then get caught out badly when a boy arrives and each parent will panic that the other is secretly disappointed. Rehearse names of both sexes and, even then, wait to see what your new baby actually looks like before making a final decision.

Not all babies suit the name you have chosen and it rapidly becomes too late to change it. Don't enjoy a joke (which might take the form of an old family name) at your child's expense – if you have to include an unfashionable family name, put it second or third. Remember to consider the impact of infelicitous initials, shortenings and derived nicknames – you will probably know someone whose parents obviously didn't.

Even if the two of you are able to agree on a shortlist of names, you will need to be prepared for the inevitable shock-horror reactions of your family. Unless you really want their opinions, it is usually best not to tell them your shortlist until your baby has been born and you have made a final decision.

# CIRCUMCISION

Bear in mind that most hospitals and most paediatricians nowadays are not in favour of routine circumcision for newborn boys, nor is it something which is usually available through the National Health Service, so if you want your baby boy circumcised you will need to make private arrangements. (Ask your GP.)

Think about it ahead of time and talk it over with your husband. Some circumcised fathers take it for granted that their son will also be circumcised. Conversely, some wives of circumcised men assume, wrongly, that their husbands will automatically want a circumcised son. If you both view circumcision as a religious imperative then fine; if only one of you does, that's awkward and needs talking through.

Although there are findings suggesting that circumcision can offer a little protection against sexually acquired infections (including HIV), it is a painful and stressful process for a baby (and not completely safe), so it seems only humane that an operation for such reasons be postponed until a teenage boy or young adult can make the decision for himself.

# CHAPTER 5:
## Fathers

### 'He was great for the first two weeks'

At an optimistic guess you will have at least dipped into most of the other chapters, even though they all seem rather replete with references to 'mothers', but this section is particularly for you. You will realise that your role is largely supportive – but it is incredibly important. The need for support seems endless (it runs into months) but this long haul is what really counts. It is a more difficult role than most men anticipate, especially as it seems to go unacknowledged.

## GETTING YOUR NEW FAMILY SAFELY HOME

This bit is good. It is an event that you will both remember for the rest of your lives, and you will be concerned to get things right. Clear your day for it if you have a chance to plan ahead, though it has to be said that it may well be on the same day of the birth, which can in turn follow a sleepless night. You may only be able to nip home for a couple of hours to fetch things and make necessary preparations.

Before leaving the house:

- Turn the central heating on (if appropriate) and up a notch so that, for the first day, the house temperature is about 20°C.
- Check that the house is as clean and tidy as possible. New mothers tend to be fairly obsessional about everything being spotless.
- Change the bed linen if her waters broke in bed.

You will have to bring:

- The baby's car seat.
- Clean clothes for the baby, including a hat: best to put these in a carrier bag in the car seat.
- Quite a lot of cash for the hospital car park (discharge arrangements can last for ever).
- Anything else your wife has asked you to bring.

However bizarre it sounds, the law in Britain states that a baby in a car must go in a child's car seat, so mothers are no longer officially allowed to travel home sitting in the back of the car holding their baby. If you order a taxi, the same applies. Therefore, before you leave, check you know how to fix your baby's car seat safely into your car (or a taxi). If your wife has been discharged from hospital only hours after giving birth, her stitches will not allow her to stand for long enough to do this herself or to read the manual and give you instructions.

At the other end, before leaving hospital, you will also have to work out how to get your baby strapped safely into the car seat. This is easiest if you take the car seat up to the ward with you, so you can work out how to put your baby into it while your wife is getting ready. Here you have time to adjust the shoulder straps (which go over rather than under your baby's shoulders) so that they are tight enough, and also to work out how to fit the crutch strap between the legs of a swaddled baby. Newly-delivered mothers cannot usually make any decisions, so your wife might not be as much help as you would ordinarily expect.

Make sure your wife doesn't leave hospital without a supply of effective pain-killers – or at least a prescription for some – especially if she has had a Caesarean. Find out what she has been getting and don't be fobbed off if staff tell you that paracetamol is all she will need once she is home.

The hospital may arrange for a nurse to carry your baby to the car, otherwise it will be you who takes your wife and your baby down to the exit. You need to keep in mind that her stitches will probably not let her walk at a normal pace – and if she has had a Caesarean section she will only be able to walk **very slowly indeed**. If the car is parked some way away, it is best to leave both her and your baby in the reception area while you collect the car to save her further walking.

New fatherhood inevitably ensures that the drive home will be cautious.

Most new parents find it better to return home without anybody else waiting for them there (see Chapter 3), but of course this isn't practical for everyone. It goes without saying that you will certainly not have organised a surprise party.

As soon as you can, get your wife and your baby into the bedroom and your wife into her night-gear and back into bed. This is really important, even if she seems to be on a high. Your task is now to monitor visitors, take the endless stream of phone calls and keep up her confidence on the feeding front (see Chapter 9). Every mother says that the most helpful thing their husband did when they returned home was 'shielding me from visitors'.

## THE EARLY WEEKS

From then on, things turn into a bit of a slog, albeit with some bits of magic. As a general outline:

- Weeks one to three will be characterised by broken nights and an increasingly sleep-deprived wife.
- Weeks three to 11 will still be characterised by broken nights, but added to this a seemingly unending series of evenings after work with a crying baby. Your increasingly sleep-deprived wife may also become tearful. But during this time your baby will become a real person who will greet you with a dazzling smile that will fill you with joy and pride.
- Weeks 11 to 14 will pose a problem for you in terms of balancing a number of issues: work versus time with baby versus support for wife versus help with baby etc., while feeling pretty tired and occasionally wondering whether it will ever end. But from now on, everything gets better.

## NIGHTS

Babies don't, unfortunately, sleep through the night until they are about four months old, by which time most couples are exhausted.

If you have a baby who is awake for large chunks of the night you may become as exhausted as your wife. This can be a bit of a nightmare, as you are now expected to be back at work in full swing just as you had imagined things were going to be a lot better.

If you are lucky enough to have another room to sleep in, it would seem sensible for you to remove yourself for the occasional night so that you are out of earshot – especially if she is breast-feeding and there is nothing much for you to do at such times. This might sound rather unhelpful on the support front, but frankly, there is absolutely no point in both parents being deprived of sleep needlessly. You will obviously discuss this with her first, rather than just inexplicably vanishing to the spare room or sofa.

Once you are back at work you need to keep up your strength to function properly there, and to enable you to be in a fit state to support your wife at weekends. Although popular belief has it that maternal fatigue gets better after the first couple of weeks, in fact most new mothers become progressively more sleep-deprived as the weeks go by, reaching their lowest point at around 10 weeks.

# EVENINGS

In the early weeks, you may want (and be able) to come home from work early so you can see your baby in the evenings. This is really helpful, as you can take your baby so that your wife can wash her hair or perhaps sort out supper (actually, anything rather than look after the baby). Between the age of three weeks and 10 weeks most babies tend to cry in the evenings, and it is wonderful for a new mother to pass the bundle over to someone else.

But if your baby develops severe evening fretting or colic, the evenings can become a strain as the weeks go by. You can find yourself in a situation that becomes really grim: when, feeling terminally exhausted yourself, you turn into your street (with a briefcase full of work) to see your wife at the window, the baby in her arms, waiting for you to come home.

You may then find that when you open the front door there is absolutely no sign of supper and you are supposed to look enthusiastic when you are handed a crying baby. You know that you are expected to walk up and down for a two-hour stretch with this crying baby. The briefcase full of work is still there and you realise that you have no clean shirts for tomorrow. It is important to remember that this is all very normal and doesn't indicate that you have a defective wife or an out-of-control baby. Grit your teeth, try to suppress any understandable irritation and hang on in there ... This is what is meant by long-term support. This is the bit that your wife will really appreciate and remember years later.

Understandably, many men like to come home from work and play with their new baby – especially when he gets beyond the crying stage and becomes so rewarding. But at around 14 weeks a problem starts. At this age, most babies need to go to bed at a reasonable time – between 7 p.m. and 8 p.m. Whatever you may think (or hope), it's not at all helpful for you to expect your baby to still be up, so that when you come back from work you can have a protracted play together. This is when you might have to be self-sacrificing, by understanding that hyping up an already tired infant makes him over-tired and impossible for you to settle, so that you have to hand him back to your wife much later on in the evening. If your work hours mean that it's not possible for you to see your baby in the week-day evenings, it really won't damage the long-term relationship between you and him.

## WEEKENDS AND SOCIALISING

Consider how best to use precious weekend time. It is probably a better short-term investment for you to take your baby out during the day so your wife can have a nap, rather than all three of you going off on a marathon expedition to Ikea.

Try to avoid long weekend drives to visit your baby's grandparents. This can be diplomatically tricky, as grandparents (and immobile great-grandparents) are likely to be keen to see as much as possible of their new grandchild. As it is difficult to catch up on the household chores and shopping if you are not at home, it may be better if they come and visit you, but this obviously needs to be discussed between yourselves before either of you make an impulsive, unilateral arrangement under pressure.

Grandparents may have somehow forgotten that small babies do not sleep through the night, so it might be worth you tactfully reminding them that what you would appreciate most is them taking the baby for a walk so you can both catch up on some sleep.

Be very wary of going out to parties during the first 10 weeks – they can go on too long and, when you eventually come home, one of you will invariably have to spend time settling your baby when all you can think of is your bed.

## WORK COMMITMENTS

It is wise to recognise some constraints:

- For the first eight weeks it will be extremely difficult for your wife (and baby) to attend formal work functions.

- In the early weeks, do not expect her to do any mega-entertaining, apart perhaps from good friends who are relaxing to be with and who are no effort.
- During the first three months you should only go to work meetings in the evening if they are absolutely essential.

# YOUR WIFE

Sophisticated men know that women fall powerfully in love with their babies and at some stage their husbands are going to feel left out. Even if you fully understand this and are braced for it, when it happens you are likely to find it a bit irritating and possibly hurtful. 'Primary maternal pre-occupation' is a state of mind which a mother acquires soon after she has delivered (or before) so that she is tuned in to her baby. She will think, talk, sleep and dream baby. No other topic (let alone your day at the office) will be of any interest to her whatsoever. It might be helpful to remind yourself that this is a temporary state, is necessary for your baby and will pass in time.

The other issue that might cross your mind is that the woman you fell in love with may seem to have had a slight personality change. During the first few weeks after giving birth, it is not uncommon for a woman to lose some of her self-confidence, and become more emotionally dependent on you, uncharacteristically indecisive and perhaps tearful. She will be extremely emotionally vulnerable.

You might in desperation think that your wife has now become simply someone's mother and has forgotten that she is also your partner. A new baby and a rip-roaring sex life do not go hand in hand, and you may privately wonder if things will ever be the same again.

The saying that having a baby cements a relationship is misleading; having a baby puts a marriage under stress. This can ultimately strengthen it but may alternatively expose a weakness – strong marriages will become stronger, but unstable ones may start to flounder.

## STAYING INVOLVED
## (IN SPITE OF EVERYTHING)

Things often get tough. You want to do your best to help, but you have to be realistic about what is actually helpful, rather than what is nice and involving for you. This means you will need to ask your wife specifically what she would appreciate from you.

Many of the most helpful things are not at all interesting – such as pacing the floors with a screaming infant at two in the morning when you are on your knees with exhaustion, and you have the most appalling work schedule the next day. Neither is wheeling the baby in the pram to Marks & Spencer at the weekend for more instant suppers while your wife has a nap. Not to mention changing the very disgusting nappies, as opposed to just the wet ones.

Another opportunity to support your wife may be to give an occasional night feed to your baby – even if he is breast-fed. Incidentally, breast-fed babies can (and should) be given expressed milk via a bottle occasionally, as it is important that they learn to use a teat.

But there are some things, such as coming home early from work so you can have a bath with your baby, which are really helpful to her, and great for your relationship with you and your baby. And it is this sort of direct involvement that is so satisfying.

# PART TWO:
## In Hospital

# CHAPTER 6:

## The first hour or so after birth

This is not a book about the birth process – which is covered in pregnancy books – so we will skip the details of labour and move to the moment of birth.

When your baby takes his first breaths he may cry, but some babies do not. In the old days, babies were hung upside down and slapped on the bottom to drain any fluid from their nose or mouth and shock them into breathing. This made all of them cry, which reassured their parents (but not, obviously, the babies). Your baby may not cry but still be perfectly well.

Newborn babies look a bit blue and lifeless before they take their first breath. Don't panic. They do not turn pink until they have taken a few breaths, and even then will probably look fairly blotchy for an hour or two, often with blue hands and feet.

At this stage your baby is still attached to the afterbirth (placenta) by the umbilical cord, which will continue to pulsate for up to two or three minutes after birth. If the baby is fine there is some advantage in waiting for these pulsations to stop or weaken as he thus gets extra blood from the placenta. The midwife will clamp the cord close to his tummy button with two plastic clips, then cut it between the clips. This does not hurt him or you. Incidentally, how the cord is clamped or by whom it is cut has no influence on the eventual shape of the tummy button. The midwife may ask your husband if he would like to cut the cord and whether he takes her up on that is entirely up to him; he certainly shouldn't feel he has to.

The midwife is very likely to suggest that you and your baby have some skin-to-skin contact because this is currently thought to be a good thing and help promote breast-feeding and your relationship. (See also page 18.) It might. More realistically and sensitively, it depends on what you want and how it's done. Placing a newborn baby on your bare stomach while a short cord continues to pulsate is fine for some mothers but not for all. Cuddling him in your arms, skin-to-skin, is only feasible if you are delivering without a gown or T-shirt on. Undressing in order to cuddle can be tricky if you are wearing a gown and have a drip in your arm. If you blanch at the thought of being handed your naked newborn, it is OK to say no. For many women all this emphasis on early skin contact feels remote and pointless compared with holding your own baby (nude or wrapped) close to you, so the two of you can gaze at each other. By the way, there is no rush about any of this. The first few minutes are not crucial for your longer-term relationship. **It doesn't matter exactly what you do so long as it feels right for you at the time.**

If you have a Caesarean birth, the baby will be handed to you over the screen and you will not have very long to hold him before having to hand him over to your husband. The obstetrician will need to remove the placenta and close the wound as soon as possible. It is usually not feasible for a woman to hold her baby while her stomach is being stitched up. She will look at him in her husband's arms.

# CHECKING THE BABY

Very soon after your baby is born he will be examined quickly, and given an Apgar score out of 10. This is a way of checking that he is in good shape and doesn't require any special help from the paediatricians. It will be repeated at five minutes. The score is based on the observation of:

- heart rate
- colour
- breathing
- muscle tone
- reflex response.

Only a few babies score a perfect 10 at one minute after birth but most score eight to 10 at five minutes. Babies born by emergency Caesarean section tend to score a bit low because they will have experienced difficulties during labour, which prompted the Caesarean in the first place. If the score is low, he may be given oxygen for a few minutes. The score is about his present condition and isn't meant to tell you anything about his future development or health as he grows up.

He is then swaddled (because babies get cold quickly), and name tags are put on his wrist and/or ankle and checked with yours before he is given back to you. Sometime during the first hour or two he will be weighed and his head and body length measured – but there is no rush about this.

At some stage in the first day or so, sometimes quite early, he will be given an injection of vitamin K to prevent haemorrhagic disease of the newborn, a rare but critical condition in which the baby's blood fails to clot so that he bleeds internally (and sometimes fatally) for a few days or weeks after birth. It is possible to give the vitamin K as a drop on the tongue, but this is less used now because it needs a follow-up drop a month later which is sometimes hard to organise. There is no truth in the old story that injected vitamin K is a risk factor for leukaemia.

# YOU

Immediately after your baby is born you may find yourself in tears of joy and relief, but you are not abnormal if this does not happen. Quite commonly it is the father who is in tears – and surprised at himself – while the mother is saying, 'Where's the tea?' If this happens, fathers are sometimes worried that their wife isn't 'bonding', but human feelings are much more complex than that. What it probably means is that she is exhausted and thirsty. It is interesting that the magic of birth not uncommonly affects fathers first and mothers a little later; while the men are coming down from their high, the mothers are warming up for theirs. Watching your baby being born is a remarkable privilege for fathers and can be a more powerful emotional experience than actually giving birth. Indeed, they may be so excited that they will not sleep and want to tell others all about it. With this in mind, they need to think in advance about whether they will need someone to share their experience (and a drink) with once they go home.

The first thought in your mind is likely to be 'Is my baby normal?' Nearly all (97 per cent) are, but you may not be prepared for what a normal newborn baby looks like:

- wet
- maybe a bluish colour at first
- perhaps a little blood on him — this will be your blood rather than his

- slippery because of a covering of a creamy substance called vernix
- rather loose reddish skin if premature
- possibly an oddly shaped head, sometimes alarmingly so
- a puffy face, especially if born face-to-pubes
- huge scrotum or large labia, and sometimes breast development (all as a result of the temporary effect of your hormones which have crossed the placenta)
- quite often fine hair on temples, forehead, shoulders and back
- sometimes small red 'stork's beak' marks on the back of the neck, on the nose or eyelids
- occasionally the 'wrong' colour hair (blond children are often born with dark hair).

Over the next few days and weeks, all these unexpected features will fade. Difficult or protracted deliveries leave their own marks, which will also disappear. The skull bones are free to move as the baby progresses through the mother's pelvis, so the fact that a baby's head may seem asymmetrical does not mean that he has brain damage and in no way indicates that he requires emergency treatment from a cranial osteopath. Forceps can leave temporary bruising marks on the cheeks and a ventouse (suction) delivery often leaves a ring mark with some swelling on the scalp. There may be a small mark on his head if a blood sample has been taken from it during labour, or a monitor clip has been attached. All these marks will vanish completely.

After reading this you might think that you will feel squeamish about your new baby (and many pregnant women secretly worry about just this) but he will actually be cuddly, very appealing and smell nice. **New babies are good news.**

Your midwife may encourage you to put your baby to the breast, as the suckling will help your uterus to contract down and also kick-start the process of lactation. Even if you have decided to bottle-feed from the start, this is still a very good idea (if you can face it and are not too exhausted). Although it is assumed that this is a natural activity, it is common to feel worried or self-conscious the first time you put your baby to the breast. You may find it difficult to hold the baby and find a comfortable position if you have a drip in your arm.

You may also feel nervous about holding him safely and generally getting things right. Fathers need to recognise that it often feels a bit awkward when neither of you have done it before, and realise that mothers, however experienced they may be with other people's babies, are likely to feel vulnerable, self-conscious and lacking in self-confidence when it comes to their own first baby. Although it is true that most new babies suck strongly in the first hour or so, be prepared for the fact yours just might not, yet still be perfectly normal.

## DELIVERING THE PLACENTA

A few minutes after the baby is born the placenta is delivered and taken away. It has done its job, and neither you nor your baby needs it any longer. It slips away from you painlessly but somewhat messily, looking like a large lump of raw liver. Before it is delivered there will have been virtually no blood or anything that might make anyone feel squeamish but, at this stage, fathers who do not like the sight of blood should stay at the head end of the bed. The same applies if you need any stitching up afterwards.

We are not very sold on the idea of eating your own placenta, cooked or not. There was a short-lived fad for this some years ago based on the observation that a number of mammals do so in order to avoid detection by predators and to conserve nutrition. Neither reason seems particularly relevant today.

# AFTERWARDS

If you have had an episiotomy (a small cut to widen the vaginal opening) or a tear you will need stitches. These are put in by a midwife or doctor using a local anaesthetic, or by topping up the epidural if you have had one. While this is being done, your feet may be put up in stirrups (slings attached to upright poles at the end of the bed) so that the stitcher can see what she or he is doing. The stitching should not be painful; if it is, say so! No one wants you to suffer, and the stitcher can adjust the local anaesthetic. Alternatively you can keep going with the gas and air. **Fathers should take responsibility for checking that you are pain-free,** as many women feel that, having coped with childbirth, they ought to be able to manage the lesser pain of stitching and don't want to cause a fuss by complaining. Nevertheless, insufficient pain relief can result in a traumatic memory that can and should always be avoided.

᠁ ⚥ Once the stitches are in, it is a good idea to attempt five short, quick pelvic floor lifts while the anaesthetic is still working. This won't burst the stitches; in fact, it will bring the stitch line together and help healing (if you manage to get any movement at all).

# A PERFECT START

When the delivery activities are over you will be helped to wash and change into a clean nightie and given a sanitary pad, since you will continue to lose quite a lot of blood and blood-stained fluid (lochia) from where the placenta was attached to your uterus. The amount of this bleeding can be surprising – it is prudent not to put on your best nightie. You will be given a cup of tea and something to eat (probably not as much as you would like, so tuck into anything you have brought with you). At this point your midwife might also suggest you go and have a shower, but this is not at all compulsory. If you feel you would rather stay with your baby, say so.

Although he will have been alert and looking around when he was born, your baby is likely to be quiet now. He may even fall asleep, and you will have an hour or so to rest together. Make the most of this. It is usually a magical time for you both as a couple. The important thing is that you now have your baby. However, it is only fair to say that it is not uncommon for some women to experience violent shivering or to be sick directly after birth, which obviously means the magic bit will have to wait.

Take some photographs: these will be so precious to you later.

Only when you are settled should the father leave you and make the necessary phone calls. Correct protocol is for him to phone your mother before his – it may prove surprisingly important that he gets this right!

# CHAPTER 7:

## The postnatal ward

After your baby has been born and you have been tidied up you will be moved to a bed in a hospital postnatal ward. Your stay in hospital will be short – possibly quite a lot shorter than you had imagined. First-time mothers who have had straightforward deliveries normally stay in hospital for a few hours, and certainly no longer than two days unless there are complications. A lot depends on the time of day you gave birth; luckily you won't be discharged during the night. Mothers who have had a Caesarean section generally stay in hospital for two to five days.

Your baby will be in a cot beside you and probably lying quietly. You can, in theory, sleep. In practice, you probably won't, as you will still be on a high following the birth, or panicking about your new responsibilities and what you're supposed to do if your baby cries. In fact, you may find that you cannot relax at all – if your baby is asleep you are worried he might not be OK and if he sneezes you are tempted to press the panic button.

If you are lucky enough to doze off you will be woken promptly by the crying of somebody else's baby, or the arrival in the ward of another recently delivered mother and the associated commotion. Be prepared to spend much of the first night (and subsequent nights) awake. Thirty years ago, a newly-delivered and exhausted mother would have been given a sleeping pill and the baby taken to the nursery to be looked after by nurses for the night; possibly a good idea but now outrageously unfashionable.

If you have had an epidural it may have weakened the control over your leg muscles, so be wary of going to the loo on your own unless you have been told that it is safe for you to do so.

# STITCHES

Your pelvic floor is likely to feel rather sore. How sore will obviously depend on how easily your baby was delivered. Some women will have an intact (though stretched) pelvic floor, but most will have stitches. The number of stitches you may have varies enormously, depending on the size and position of your baby during delivery. At one end of the spectrum you may have a couple of stitches following a small tear, and at the other extreme it might seem that your entire pelvic floor is stitched up.

Most forceps deliveries necessitate an episiotomy, and different types of forceps require different-sized cuts and therefore different numbers of stitches. If the woman in the next bed to you claims that she had forceps yet is leaping around with alarming agility while you can't sit down, don't panic that something has gone wrong; she probably simply had a less complicated delivery. You may also have developed a thrombosed external pile (peri-anal haematoma), which is a burst blood vessel under the skin around the anus. This can be appallingly painful but will usually clear up within 10 days without needing any treatment. Meanwhile it may help to lie on your side or on your back with your bottom on a pillow for as much of the time as possible.

If your labour was long and you had a difficult second stage, you might find you have aching or sore muscles just about everywhere. You may even discover that you have bloodshot eyes (especially if you were dozing in the antenatal class that concentrated on 'pushing' properly). Don't worry – you will recover.

# MANAGING A PAINFUL PELVIC FLOOR

Things will get better! When offered pain relief, take it if you need it. You will be offered something, perhaps paracetamol, which is compatible with breast milk. No hospital is going to give you medicines that will harm your baby.

**Continue your pelvic floor exercises** (see page 127 if you don't know how) even if you have had a Caesarean section (as soon as your catheter is out).

Do them in groups of five contractions (flicks) each time, 10 times a day (making a total of 50 contractions a day) however sore your stitches are and even if you have got painful external piles. At this stage it is not necessary to hold the contraction for any longer than a couple of seconds at a time. Your muscles will feel rather 'spongy' at first, due to swelling in the area, especially if you have had a lot of stitches. The exercises help the healing process by increasing the blood supply to the area and dispersing the swelling.

Any increase in intra-abdominal pressure will put a strain on your stitches and already-stretched pelvic floor muscles, so try to remember to tighten your muscles whenever you cough, sneeze, laugh or get up from sitting. If you are in a lot of pain, ask to see a specialist obstetric physiotherapist (whose formal title is a physiotherapist in women's health) who will have been trained to help with stitch and bottom problems.

At some stage (usually 24 hours after delivery) you are going to have to face the daunting task of opening your bowels. You may well be at home by then and grateful to be able to use your own loo. Physiotherapists often call this the fourth stage of labour – you may discover that you are in agreement with them. Most women are fairly constipated after having had a baby, which doesn't make things any easier. This is because slight constipation in pregnancy is common and worsened by mild dehydration during labour. The best thing you can do is drink plenty of fluid after the birth and keep up your intake of fruit (kiwi fruit and figs have a good reputation).

You are likely to worry that you will be unable to open your bowels without splitting your stitches and having the world fall out of your bottom. You can counter this apprehension and protect your pelvic floor muscles if you support your stitch-line when you bear down. Take a fresh sanitary/maternity pad into the loo with you, fold it in half and hold it against your stitches as you gently try to push down.

## AFTER A CAESAREAN SECTION

Every time you try to move, your tummy muscles will hurt. This includes getting in and out of bed, walking, laughing, sobbing, coughing or going to the loo. It will help if you either try to **contract your tummy muscles or support them with your hand before doing any of the above.**

The amount of pain that women experience is variable – and there is a big difference between having an elective Caesarean (less pain) and an emergency Caesarean after a long labour (more pain). Under no circumstances refuse painkillers when you are offered them, because **pain will slow your recovery.** You really need the expertise of a physiotherapist to help you move around. If there isn't one available, try the following suggestions:

- Ensure your bed height is as high as possible. Hospital beds are adjustable – but you may have to ask a member of staff to show you how to raise it if it isn't obvious. It should be high enough to make it easy for you to put your feet onto the floor with your legs as straight as possible when you are perched on the side of the bed.
- When trying to get out of bed: use the electric back-rest (if there is one) to move you to an upright sitting position. Shuffle your bottom to the edge and lift one leg at a time over the side, using your hands to lift the leg if necessary. Separate your knees, support your wound with a hand, lean forwards and slowly stand up.
- Getting successfully back into bed means lowering your bottom onto an exact position on the mattress.
  - If you want to get back into the sitting position, lower your bottom halfway across the width of the mattress and as near to the pillows as possible. Again, lift one leg at a time, using your hands if necessary.
  - When you want to get back into bed and lie down, lower your bottom onto the mattress, halfway down its length, pull in your tummy and drop quickly sideways onto the pillows – your legs and feet will follow.

The point of all this is to avoid the difficulty of shifting around once in bed.

You should not be expected to lift your baby out of his crib or get in and out of bed on your own while carrying him. Ask a midwife (or more realistically, your husband or another mother) to hand you your baby, until you feel confident.

Sometimes women experience frightening stomach cramps, especially when they stand up and walk. Don't panic that something has been left behind – it is most likely to be trapped wind, which will eventually pass through. Surprisingly, this same wind can also result in pain behind the right shoulder. This will disappear within a day or so.

## PICKING UP YOUR BABY

Don't be inhibited about this. Pick up your baby when you feel like it and cradle his head with your fingers to support it as you do so.

He needs to be handled and get to know you. Within the first few days he learns to recognise your face, voice and smell, and will respond to you more than any other person. Your face is his first plaything and, in a few weeks' time, you will see his smile when he sees you and you talk to him. Start on it now: pick him up and talk to him in a light tone, using any silly phrase that comes to mind. Tell him what you think of him or what is going on – it doesn't really matter what you say, but a high-pitched, sing-song voice will appeal to him. Get him used to the sound of you. Pull faces at him so that he learns all the appearances of your face. Kiss and cuddle him. You won't damage anything, nor will you 'spoil' him by picking him up.

Some things about your baby might alarm you:

- His umbilical stump and its clip may look distinctly off-putting and about to snap off dangerously. It won't. It will separate gradually, usually dropping off within the first 10 days. The midwives will show you how to clean it. Most mothers try to fold the top of the nappy below it so that urine doesn't seep into the umbilical area, but it is not a disaster if it does, and you don't need special nappies with a cut-out section for the cord area.
- Newborn babies have little control over their heads, which roll around and need supporting by your fingers as you pick them up.
- Although you probably knew that a baby has two soft patches (fontanelles) in his skull, it is a bit of a jolt when you feel them for the first time. There is a membrane under the skin which is much tougher than it feels, and you won't puncture it by accident.
- A scalp monitor may leave a small scab of dried blood on the top of your baby's head, a ventouse can leave a circular mark and forceps can occasionally produce bruise marks or scratches on his face. These will disappear completely.
- Many newborn babies appear to have a squint. This becomes less evident as they learn to co-ordinate their eye movements.
- Their first bowel movement is greenish-black and sticky; this is meconium, which fills the bowels of babies in the womb. If there is a pink or orange (or, in girls, a bloody) stain in the nappy, this is probably normal, but check with your midwife.

# GIVING YOUR BABY COLOSTRUM

Babies don't need milk, or much in the way of calories, for the first three days, but they do need fluid. They are born with a good reserve supply of nutrition. It is not uncommon for them to lose up to 10 per cent of their birth weight in the first five days and nature budgets for this. Babies vary enormously during these early days. Some are very sleepy and are quite uninterested in feeding; others are keen to suckle immediately and seem to be starving. Unfortunately, you are likely to worry on both counts.

Your milk won't begin to come through until around three or four days after delivery (occasionally longer). (See page 109.) You do, however, need to put your baby to the breast before then, and, even if he is very sleepy, don't leave it longer than 12 hours after delivery before doing so. Before they start producing milk – in fact, before your baby is born – your breasts produce a small amount of yellowish fluid called colostrum. This contains antibodies against infection as well as other goodies and is, from the baby's point of view, very important. The suckling of your baby will also help stimulate the release of hormones that kick-start the lactation process (though if, for any reason, you can't put your baby to the breast the milk will still come through).

Try to find an experienced midwife to help you. Just because your baby suckled successfully after birth doesn't mean he or you will know exactly what to do next time. Latching on is a skill to be learned and requires practise. Whoever you are able to enlist needs to be there to ensure your baby is latching on properly, taking both the nipple and the areola (brown area around it) into his mouth rather than hanging on to the nipple only, which will make it sore. He needs to be able to breathe as well as suck – so don't hold him so close that your breast is over his nose.

You will get sore nipples if you try to pull your baby off while he is still sucking, so your midwife can show you how to get him to release your nipple as well. You do this by parting his gums with your little finger. If your baby is uninterested in feeding you may be told (even threatened!) that your milk won't come in unless he suckles all the time. In fact it will. In some cultures the baby isn't put to the breast until the mother begins to lactate.

You are also likely to worry that he isn't getting enough colostrum if he wants to suckle all the time. Actually, nature tends to get things right, providing enough colostrum (in teaspoon quantities) to keep him going until your milk comes through. You don't have to give your baby a bottle of formula milk in the first three days unless this is on the specific advice of a paediatrician. There is a risk that giving an impatient baby a bottle of formula milk when it is not nutritionally required will fill him up and make him less prepared to suckle at the breast when your milk does come through. There are four main exceptions to this:

1. Babies who have not grown adequately during pregnancy are sometimes initially unable to regulate their own blood sugar level well enough and need extra feeding.

2. Very big babies sometimes can't settle at all because they are genuinely starving. A paediatrician can tell you if this is the case.

3. If you have already developed horribly sore nipples by day two, you may have no alternative but to rest them for a feed or two, by using formula milk.

4. Some women simply do not produce colostrum and their baby will need formula milk until their milk comes through.

But, having said this, it is quite possible that some midwives will strenuously oppose, even forbid (!) bottle-feeding in the above emergencies and insist on protracted yet futile breast-suckling. We know this sometimes happens. Occasionally it seems this is because they or their hospital misinterpret the Baby-Friendly initiative which is a laudable attempt to promote breast-feeding internationally by UNICEF and the World Health Organization (see www.babyfriendly.org.uk). However, it is not supposed to be a rigid doctrine and does not in any way extend to prohibiting or condemning bottle-feeding. We fail to see how with-holding necessary food from a baby can in any way be regarded as 'baby-friendly'. Do not be intimidated if you think your baby is starving and needs formula milk – insist on seeing a senior paediatrician who will ascertain if this is the case.

Such crises are not common. The chances are that you and your baby will start to get into the swing of breast-feeding during the first three days. If you are still in hospital, brace yourself for the near-certainty that each professional you see will give you different advice on technique. In fact, you will be amazed that there is so much different advice to be had. Every mother finds this particularly confusing and unsettling.

Most babies will be able to take all the colostrum they need by suckling five to 10 minutes on each breast every three hours or so. Using only one breast for each feed at this stage is nonsense. Unlike breast milk, which contains fore and hind milk (see page 115), there is no 'fore' and 'hind' colostrum.

If he seems to want to suckle for much longer periods, hear warning bells. It's probable that he's not getting enough colostrum because his positioning is incorrect.

This means that, although he may be properly latched on to the nipple and areola, he is not on at the correct angle to the breast. This results in kinking of the tiny ducts inside the breast and nipple which blocks the flow of the colostrum. He will suck but probably won't be swallowing much, so wants to suck for a long time, and you are in danger of getting sore nipples before you have even started to lactate (see page 118). Once again, you need the help of an expert.

## SITTING IN A COMFORTABLE POSITION TO FEED

If you have a crutch full of bruises or stitches, sitting in bed or on a chair while you are feeding may be painful, so it is worth taking the trouble to make yourself as comfortable as you possibly can. Any discomfort or pain you may be experiencing will certainly not facilitate your milk flow, and you may be sitting for half an hour or so. Some wards provide a rubber ring to sit on, but a pillow doubled over along its long axis (the opposite to how you would instinctively fold a pillow) and put under your thighs as close to your buttocks as possible is just as effective (see overleaf). Both devices take your body weight off the stitches. If you have had a Caesarean section, lying your baby on a pillow or two on your lap should take his weight off your abdominal stitch-line.

You should sit well back in the chair and support your feet on a footstool if possible. You can take the strain off your back and shoulders by supporting the baby on another pillow or two across your lap so that you are bringing baby up to breast rather than breast down to baby. Once he is latched on comfortably, try to drop your shoulders.

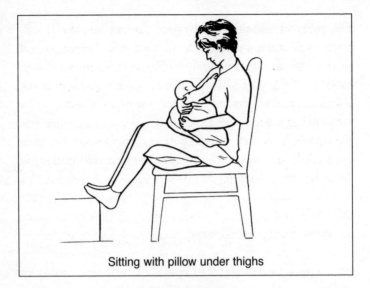

Sitting with pillow under thighs

## AFTER-PAINS

When your baby suckles, you may experience some 'after-pains', though these are more common in second-time mothers. The suckling of your baby releases hormones that make your uterus contract. This can feel just like contractions during labour and be very painful, but they do mean the uterus is contracting down properly to its pre-pregnancy size. Try the deep breathing you were taught to do for labour if this happens.

## VISITORS

This is an issue that only applies if you are kept in hospital for more than a day. The important point is that the visitors need to be regulated by your husband. We carried out a survey in which we asked new mothers about their early experiences when they had just had their baby. They said that the most helpful contribution their husbands made was shielding them from visitors. Your husband must make sure that, when he tells people about your new baby, he finds out if they plan to visit you, and if so, discusses with you whether this is what you want.

People in hospital are trapped and cannot escape the visitor who stays too long. This can apply even when you are back home. A newly-delivered mother will not enjoy the necessary courtesies of introducing elderly relatives to current mates (and sustaining the conversation), when all she really wants to do is disappear into the lavatory before tackling another feed. Nor is she going to find it easy to attempt to breast-feed in front of a well-meaning male work colleague or her father-in-law – however uninhibited she may be under normal circumstances. Husbands can try to ensure that she is not exposed to any 'surprise' visits, and that you both have enough time of your own together with your baby.

Another issue for your husband to be aware of is that women who have just had a baby don't usually look their best! A long labour may leave the newly-delivered mother looking seriously steamrollered – deathly pale, greasy-haired, blotchy, and possibly with a drip in her arm (though these are usually removed an hour or so after delivery). A day or two after delivery it is also normal for some women to find they become very sweaty, though they should *not* have a raised temperature.

Your husband is your most important visitor and there must be time for the two of you to see each other alone. The only other visitors who may be important are your parents and his; other people can visit you when you return home. It is probably wise for your husband to tell visitors that 15 minutes is enough – less for children. Pre-school children are not only exhausting but remarkably adept at preventing or interrupting conversations between their parents. They just need to check that you are all right and that there really is a baby. This doesn't take long and they become tiring if they stay longer. Give them a good hug and tell them when you'll be home. (The present from the new baby comes later, when you get home.)

## BEFORE YOU ARE DISCHARGED

Your baby should be examined by a paediatrician (or occasionally a specially trained midwife) before he leaves hospital. In practice, this may be deferred because you are sent home early. Don't be afraid to ask questions during the examination (though not while the paediatrician or midwife is listening to the heart).

# PART THREE:
## The First Six Weeks

# CHAPTER 8:

## Coming home

Coming home is the time when the support of your husband (or, if not possible or available, someone such as your mother) is particularly important. He will need to clear his day, turn up at the hospital on time with the car seat and be prepared to wait – looking outwardly calm and showing no signs of impatience. (See page 49 for more on this.)

You may be secretly nervous about the drive home but it is remarkable how new fatherhood calms even the most vigorous male driver.

When you get home, a competent husband will have already cleared up a bit, removing dirty dishes from the table and empty bottles from the kitchen. He will have guessed that you will not want to be faced with a scene suggesting that you now have the task of looking after two dependants. He will certainly not have organised a reception party.

You might want to have a cup of coffee in the kitchen and generally settle back into being at home again. (This does not mean washing the kitchen floor.) Incidentally, breast-feeding mothers are usually able to eat and drink more or less whatever they fancy, so long as it is in moderation. There are very few foods (mainly garlic, curry or sometimes citrus fruits) that will affect their babies. The amount of caffeine in the odd cup of tea or coffee is unlikely to cause trouble.

Sooner or later, change back into a nightdress or pyjamas and pile into bed with your baby by your side. Start as you mean to continue by contracting your pelvic floor while you lie in bed, resolving to do 50 a day in 10 groups of five (for the time being). You might work out a way of reminding yourself about these for the next few days until you have programmed yourself – a visible sticky note on your television/changing table/crib, for instance.

Quite possibly you will feel totally spaced-out and in a dream, which can be somewhat unsettling. This is common, is called depersonalisation, and is nothing to worry about. There isn't much that you have to do at this stage except be there for your baby. The feeling will wear off after a day or two.

A feeling of exhaustion can wash over you at any stage, especially if you are anaemic. Normally, a healthy woman has blood with a haemoglobin level of 12–14 g per 100 ml. Haemoglobin is the red pigment in blood that transports oxygen around the body. Loss of blood during and after birth will leave you anaemic with a low haemoglobin level. This is particularly likely after a Caesarean. The hospital may have checked your blood for anaemia before you go home and, if necessary, will give you a supply of iron pills. These work over a period of weeks before they are fully effective. You will feel seriously steamrollered if your haemoglobin is below 10 g per 100 ml. Incidentally, foods that contain iron are liver, red meat, leafy green vegetables and breakfast cereals containing supplements.

On the other hand, some new mothers have a manic buzz at this stage and feel they can take on the world. Having been told (or read) that they will be tired, they are on a high that this is clearly not happening to them. It's a great feeling but a bit of a nuisance because they can't sleep and tend to take on too much. It usually settles after a few days, though sometimes takes as long as a couple of weeks. Awkwardly, it means that they can't see the point of going to bed.

## LOCHIA

For the first few days you are likely to bleed alarmingly heavily from your vagina, as if you were having a very heavy period, but rather more so. This follows both Caesarean and vaginal births. Blood, perhaps with a few clots, seeps from the site where the placenta was attached to the wall of the uterus. This is painless and quite normal. The community midwife may seem oddly curious as to its quantity, colour and smell, but it is because she needs to check that all is progressing normally with no infection or bits of placenta ('retained products') left behind.

## YOUR FIRST BATH

Sweating a lot after having a baby is common, especially if you put on extra weight while pregnant. You will look forward to having a bath. Be prepared for the experience of a sinking heart the first time that you strip off and have a chance to look at yourself in private. The bulge will not yet have gone and you may appear at least three (often six) months pregnant. The skin on your tummy will look like orange-peel or rumpled crêpe paper. So it does on other women too. It will go. If you have had a Caesarean section there will be an alarming wad of flab which forms a 'shelf' above the incision. This, too, subsides with time. The linea nigra (the pigmented line running up the middle of your abdomen) is sometimes even more evident after you have had your baby than before, as are bright purple stretch marks on your lower tummy. All these will gradually fade during the next few months.

# REST

It is imperative for your long-term recovery that you get as much of this (and sleep) as possible. Try to carry on wearing night-gear and be in or around your bed for the first few days after coming home, however wonderful and exuberant you may feel. This will remind other people that you have just had a baby and are not in any way back to normal – but there are more important reasons. The old lying-in period was a very good principle (your mother would have probably been in hospital for 10 days after the birth of her first baby). It made you move into the slow lane, which is where you want to be for your own sake and in order to fall in step with your baby. This is no superficial homily; it is a necessary process of adjustment. You need a restful time in order for your body to heal and recuperate from the physical stresses of labour and delivery. Your body also has to adjust to its new, non-pregnant state and to the task of producing milk. Trying to demonstrate to the world that you have not been affected in any way by giving birth is a ridiculous idea. Do not believe the myth about women giving birth behind a bush and returning to work in the fields half an hour later.

## (STEP-) BROTHERS AND SISTERS

If you have other children, they will want to see you and the new baby. Try not to introduce him to them while you are feeding – it will upset them if they think they have been displaced in your affections. If the baby has brought them a present (see page 33), now is the right time for them to have it. Make sure that you have time to talk to them and listen to their questions or accounts of what they have been doing. Tell them you will be resting in bed for several days. Let them hold the baby if they want to **but make it absolutely clear that children are not allowed to pick up the baby unless an adult is present.**

## WHERE WILL THE BABY GO?

For much of the day, he will be beside you, either by your bed or in the kitchen while you are eating. He needs to be adequately warm but not allowed to overheat. To gauge how warm he is, slip your hand inside his vest to feel his body temperature on his chest or upper back. Don't rely on feeling his hands and feet, which, in tiny babies, are quite often much colder than the rest of the body. Babies should never get so hot that they sweat.

You will get a great deal of advice on the question of where he sleeps at night. For more on this, see page 41. Most parents start by having the baby sleep in their room with them (even if they have a maternity nurse). This is usually thought to be the best place because it feels right for most parents and is recommended on safety grounds though the evidence for this is weak. The only place that is wrong is somewhere with which you don't feel comfortable, even if you have been told it is the right place.

The night temperature of the room where your baby sleeps should be neither too low nor oven-like – somewhere between 16°C and 20°C is sensible, which is warmer than some adults like (one reason why babies are eventually moved into their own rooms). You will need a convector heater or electric radiator with a thermostat. This is probably easier than running your central heating all night and turning down the temperature valves on all your other radiators. Don't put his crib next to a radiator. Although your baby will need to be warm, there are real dangers if he overheats. Unlike an older child, he cannot rearrange his duvet or stick a bare foot out from under the covers to cool himself. Never let him sleep with a hat on indoors: babies need to be able to lose heat through their heads.

You will have to feed your baby at night and may need an extra supply of pillows to prop you up if you are feeding him in your own bed.

## IN WHAT POSITION SHOULD HE SLEEP?

On his back or, if he really doesn't look comfortable like that, on his side for the first few days. The important thing is to get him into a habit of sleeping on his back as soon as you can. **Do not put him to sleep on his front.** Cot deaths have been halved since mothers were advised not to put young babies to sleep on their fronts. Place your baby with his feet near the end of the Moses basket or carrycot, so, if he manages to wriggle, he won't disappear under his top blanket.

# SWADDLING

This is an age-old practice. Small babies feel more secure and will sleep better if they are swaddled. The purpose is essentially to contain the baby's startle reflex. This is when his arms jerk up in response to a sudden sound or movement.

Swaddling also helps stabilise his temperature without overheating. There is absolutely no evidence that swaddling increases the (tiny) risk of cot death – so long as you use the right material and he is not overdressed – in spite of what you might be told.

Wrap a flannelette or brushed cotton (Winceyette) receiving/swaddling sheet firmly around the baby, including his shoulders and arms (see overleaf). The material must be non-stretchy cotton – a sheet rather than a blanket. It simply doesn't matter that he can't wave his arms around all the time for a few weeks. Your baby is too uncoordinated as yet (however gifted he may be!) to actively take his fingers or thumb to his mouth and keep them there. He won't be able to do this until he is around 14 weeks old.

# DUMMIES

Unfortunately these are unfashionable at present and often evoke cries of horror. However, dummies can be indispensable in the early weeks, especially if you have a 'sucky' or unsettled baby who finds it difficult to fall asleep.

Many people help a baby settle himself by letting him suck the tip of their little finger. It is difficult to understand why they think this is preferable to a dummy, as the obvious disadvantage of a finger is that it is attached to a person. **There is absolutely nothing wrong**

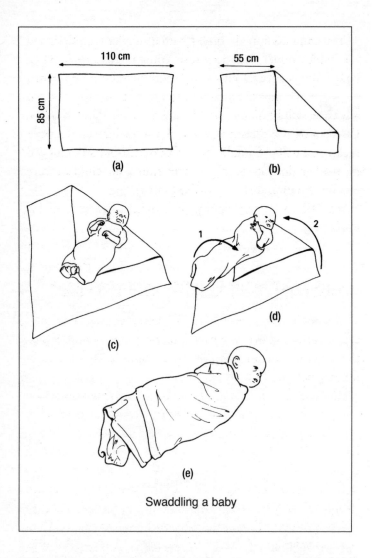

Swaddling a baby

in letting a tiny baby do what he enjoys – sucking – as long as he isn't given a dummy all the time. In any case, all parents would agree there is nothing worse than a crying (unhappy) baby. A dummy helps a baby learn self-soothing behaviour and, if it is used judiciously, he won't get dependent on it.

You can now buy dummies with a smaller teat, designed for babies under four months. You can discard it when your baby is about four or five months old – by this time, he will have developed interests beyond sucking and, in any case, will be able to find his own fingers if he wants to. Giving a baby a dummy to help him settle himself does not mean you will eventually have a two-year-old still plugged in; neither does it mean you will ruin your child's future tooth formation (ask any orthodontist).

It's OK to let your baby sleep with a dummy in his mouth.

## THE FIRST NIGHT AT HOME WITH YOUR BABY

This usually feels a bit scary. As one new father described the situation: you arrive home, unwrap the most precious thing in the world ... and realise it comes with absolutely no instructions!

But babies are pretty parent-proof and it is virtually impossible for you to do anything really dangerous. Try very hard not to get into the habit of thinking that your baby won't survive unless he is in the hands of a qualified professional.

**Go to bed early!** If you are breast-feeding, you are likely to find yourself thirsty (and probably hungry) while feeding in the night, so it may be sensible to lay in appropriate provisions in advance. Unless he has unwisely drunk too much, the perfect man will wake with you for feeds, and can usefully bring you up a cup of tea as required. Having him with you for your first night feed out of hospital is a real help and confidence booster. Make the most of all this; it is not guaranteed to last, especially when he is back at work.

Babies don't always make it easy for you and may choose their first night out of all other options to refuse to settle after a feed. This may be because you had a celebratory glass of champagne, which a number of babies don't seem to like (in any case, red wine is better for you because of its iron content). If he cries instead of settling after a feed, keep calm and assume it is wind. His father should pick him up and walk him round for 15 minutes or so rubbing his back. If this doesn't work, he should try wrapping him up reasonably tightly (see page 92) and putting him down, rhythmically joggling his crib or basket, again for at least 15 minutes. If all else fails, he will have to walk round the room with his baby over his shoulder for as long as it takes. He may find it unsettling to discover that there isn't an 'off' button for crying. Sometimes one simply has to try and keep as calm as possible and hang on in there.

Worse than refusing to settle, you may find your baby seems to be starving and, in spite of apparently feeding perfectly in hospital, has now apparently completely forgotten how to suck. You are both distraught and seriously sleep-deprived with a hysterical, screaming baby – and it is two o'clock in the morning. You are terrified that there is something wrong and your baby will suddenly stop breathing or scream himself into a fit (he won't), and you simply don't know what to do.

If you really can't get him latched on to the breast, as a last resort you may have no alternative but to offer him previously boiled warm water or 25 ml of formula milk from a bottle or, if you don't have one, a teaspoon. (Do not use a cup with a screaming baby; he may inhale fluid.) This should at least allow you all to get some sleep and end a panic-inducing crisis. But however apprehensive you may feel, make sure you offer your baby the breast again when he wakes up and everyone is calmer. Otherwise you are both in danger of going into a downward spiral of losing confidence and feeling that neither of you is ever going to master the art of sucking or feeding.

# POSSIBLE MEDICAL PROBLEMS

Now you are at home, and away from on-tap medical support, you need to know what to take seriously. Mothers are so concerned about their new infant that they often don't think about themselves, but if you notice any of the following, you need to contact your community midwife or GP as soon as possible:

## You – the newly delivered mother

- a temperature
- persistent abdominal or back pain
- pains in your chest accompanied by breathlessness
- a persistent headache, especially with vomiting or vision disturbance
- lochia that smells unpleasant – rather than like blood
- large clots of blood or sudden profuse bleeding
- a swollen, tender calf or thigh
- a feeling that you might have 'flu
- a painful or red area in your breast.

## Your baby

- a feeling you have that he is seriously unwell
- a persisting, noticeable change in the sound of his crying

- vomiting after every feed in the first few days before your milk comes through
- increasing jaundice
- having to wake your baby for every feed, which he then doesn't take, coupled with less than six wet nappies a day (a baby who doesn't pass urine will be dehydrated)
- a temperature.

# CHAPTER 9:

## The first week or so with your baby

Future success depends on taking life gently now while you and your baby are relatively relaxed (or dazed).

Your baby also needs time to recuperate from the massive physiological changes which occur at birth. New babies are generally fairly quiet for the first two or three weeks, and most spend much of their time asleep. This is their way of warding off too much stimulation, which will make them jittery. The last thing they want at this stage is to be passed around a circle of admirers who all want a 'cuddle', or over-stimulated by parents entering them for the developmental Olympics. They need some space for themselves and so do you. Don't be tempted to think that this 'good' phase will necessarily last, but do make the most of it. You need rest, not just for its own sake but for the benefit of your baby. Hyperactive new mothers will find it difficult to settle their babies into successful breast-feeding.

## YOUR HUSBAND'S CONTINUING SUPPORT

Staying in and around the bedroom will not automatically guarantee that you get any daytime sleep. Your husband must try to ensure you do get as much as possible, so at some stage during the day, he should take the baby downstairs and out of your earshot so that you can sleep undisturbed. He needs to unplug/turn off the phones, and think about putting a Post-it note on the front door asking callers not to ring the bell. He may have to remind you to think of yourself. A new mother tends to be intensely preoccupied with her baby (primary maternal preoccupation) and will tend to put his needs before her own. This can leave her exhausted.

Let your husband fetch and carry and, in suitable weather, even take your baby out in the pram. But he will need to return within an agreed time to prevent you falling into the trap of assuming only you are capable of preventing a pram from going under the wheels of a lorry. He should answer the door, take the phone calls and organise the meals. (Incidentally, he should avoid serving up very spicy foods, particularly garlic, as these can find their way into your breast milk and thus into the baby, making some babies uncomfortable and restless.)

## FOUR-DAY BLUES

On about the fourth day after birth, around the time that your milk comes through, some (a little more than half) of newly-delivered mothers find themselves in tears for trivial reasons. No one is quite sure what triggers this, but there is a fall in the level of progesterone at this time. One explanation could be that this drop in hormone level makes women more emotionally vulnerable, so that they experience a heightened sensitivity to criticism. The casual comments of visitors sound like damning indictments, and self-esteem plummets to an all-time low. If you are still in hospital this is particularly likely to happen if a healthcare professional implies that any unsuccessful breast-feeding attempts indicate that you are clearly a complete failure as a mother. Worse, if you want to (or have to) give your baby a bottle of formula milk and are unlucky enough to be exposed to a breast-feeding fanatic, you may be made to feel little better than someone who supports infanticide. Healthcare professionals are understandably keen to promote breast-feeding (as are we), but sometimes this can go too far. (See page 78.) We have heard too many reports of instances which, frankly, amount to bullying. If you are in hospital and find yourself in this situation, ask to see a consultant. If you are not up to it, ask your husband to do so.

If you have the baby blues you find it even more difficult to concentrate, and may well feel anxious or panicky as to whether you will be able to cope with your baby, followed by more weeping. This is not the real you. Nor is this postnatal depression. In fact, it isn't really depression at all but a short-lived state of emotional turmoil which passes after a few days and needs no medical treatment.

## YOUR BABY GENERALLY

During this first week he may come out in white spots over his nose and upper cheeks which are called milia. They are also sometimes called milk spots, which is misleading, as they have nothing to do with the quality or type of milk the baby is having. They are normal and will go of their own accord. Do not pick or squeeze them.

Within the week, the stump of the umbilical cord drops off (to the great relief of most mothers). Occasionally it hangs on into the second week, in which case you must continue with the routine for cleaning it that you were shown by your midwife, however squeamish you may feel. This is because it is a potential site for bacterial infection which can track up to the baby's liver. (You can recognise a bacterial infection by an unpleasant smell.) Once the cord has dropped off, no special cleaning procedure is necessary.

Tiny babies have long fingernails and will scratch their own faces. Don't be afraid to cut the nails using baby scissors while your baby is asleep. Alternatively, you can file them with an emery board – either method is more efficient than the traditional practice of nibbling them yourself.

Hiccups and sneezes are common and of no particular significance. Sometimes sneezes are triggered by bright light.

You may notice that your baby sometimes has a squint, which, if it comes and goes, doesn't usually matter at this stage. It is most likely to be a result of him not yet having learned to co-ordinate his eye movements. Obviously, a permanent squint needs investigating.

An eye infection with sticky eyelids and a discharge is something to mention to your midwife. Meanwhile, bathe the eye with sterile water (boiled water that has been cooled), wiping from the tear duct to the outside of the eye. Change the pad for the other eye. A non-conventional treatment that often works is, having done the above, to drop a little of your breast milk into his eye.

## WET AND DIRTY NAPPIES

You can expect your baby to have a wet nappy about six times a day. A baby who does not feed can get dehydrated and not pass urine so frequently. The wee he does pass may be slightly smelly. If you think this is the case, point it out to your midwife, who can check his state of hydration and alert your doctor if necessary.

The contents of your baby's first dirty nappy may be a bit of a shock: black, sticky, tar-like and copious – he seems to be up to his ears in it. This is meconium which was present in your baby's intestines before he was born. Your heart will sink at the prospect of cleaning it all up but the next stool will be yellowish and the consistency of a ripe banana. Most babies produce meconium within 24 hours of birth – if your baby hasn't done so by 36 hours, tell your midwife. From then onwards, you can expect bottle-fed babies to open their bowels daily, but the frequency of bowel movements varies enormously in breast-fed babies – anything from every nappy change to every five days. But another time to alert your midwife is if a normally yellowish stool turns green or if there is blood in the stool, as this may indicate underfeeding or even infection.

## CHANGING NAPPIES

Make sure you have a surface which is at your waist height on which to change your baby's nappy. You may be changing your baby as often as 10 times a day at this stage and you will get low backache if the changing surface is too low. It is extremely common for new mothers to develop low back pain at some stage, and bending forward to change your baby is one of the causes. If you don't have a changing table, change your baby on the bedroom floor rather than your bed.

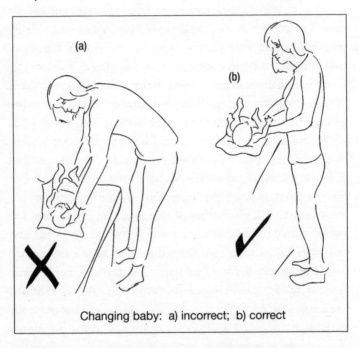

Changing baby: a) incorrect; b) correct

If you find that you have bought a changing table that is too low, block it up on books or telephone directories to bring it to the correct height. (If it is a trolley with castors, you will obviously need to unscrew the castors first.) If space allows, keep a low stool under the changing table so you can rest one foot on it while changing your baby. This stops you arching your lower back. It doesn't matter, by the way, if you stand at his feet or by his side when you change him.

If your house/flat is on two levels, think about having two changing mats, one for upstairs and one downstairs. There is no point in you carrying your baby up a flight of stairs (especially if you have had a Caesarean section) just to whip off a damp nappy. The kitchen table or sitting-room floor will do.

Cover a plastic changing mat with a muslin square (or small towel) to shield the baby from the touch of chilly vinyl. The muslin will also soak up the inevitable jet of urine and can be put straight into the washing machine.

It is easier to change your baby near running water. Breast-fed babies have fairly odourless stools, but those who are bottle-fed can put out some stinkers. If your baby has a dirty nappy, clean his bottom with warm water, using cotton wool balls. Some authorities caution against the use of soap, but Simple soap (the brand name for soap that has absolutely no additives) causes no problems in our experience. Alternatively you can use baby wipes or lotion to clean the buttocks, and run the small risk of a temporary local skin reaction developing.

After drying his bottom, most people put some barrier cream (basic zinc and castor oil cream, or a branded variant such as Sudocrem) on his buttocks. You may be told that this is unnecessary and, indeed, if your baby's bottom remains pristine without any cream, that will be true. See how you go. It is the most potent protection against nappy rash, the main cause of which tends to be leaving a baby to lounge around in a soggy nappy. It is not urine that gives a baby nappy rash, but ammonia released from old urine. Always wash your hands after changing a soiled nappy; faecal organisms get everywhere. Introduce your husband to the joys of nappy changing sooner rather than later, and praise his prowess, irrespective of your private judgement.

You will notice that boy babies have a tight foreskin. Under no circumstances try pulling this back, as it may have an attachment to the glans underneath at this stage.

# WASHING AND BATHING

Your baby won't need a bath every day but you will still need to do the following:

- Wipe both eyes from nose to ear with sterile (warm, previously boiled) water, using a separate piece of wet cotton wool for each.
- Soap under his chin, under his armpits and behind his ears.
- Pat-dry these areas carefully – they can sometimes get sore.
- A cotton bud can be useful for drying behind (not inside) his ears.

If you are going to give him a bath on his own, be very careful to go down on one knee rather than bending over while standing. The best baby baths are those which hook over the side of your bath, fill from your bath taps and have their own plug. This means that the baby is at a reasonable level and you don't have to lug gallons of water around. Check the water temperature by putting a dry hand or elbow in it: it should be distinctly warm rather than tepid.

The easiest and most fun way to bath a baby is to put him into the adult bath with his father. The water can be the usual comfortable temperature for most adults (assuming they don't like it as hot as it is possible to tolerate). When you lift him (the baby!) out, wrap him quickly in his own towel, warmed if possible.

You can still bath a baby if his cord is determined to stay attached. If you have been shown a cleaning routine for the stump, use this when you have dried him. If you have not, simply pat it dry (kitchen roll is often better than a towel, as you can throw it away rather than having to wash the towel).

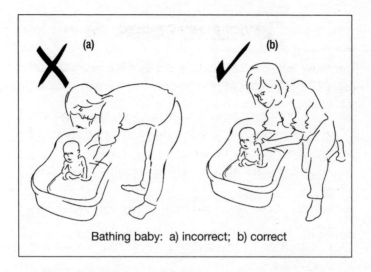

Bathing baby: a) incorrect; b) correct

Brush his hair daily and keep an eye open for cradle cap (crusty scales), which will need to be anointed with any of several lotions you can buy and subsequently worked off with a very soft toothbrush or nailbrush.

# JAUNDICE

Some babies develop mild jaundice a few days after their birth because their livers are not yet working to full capacity.

If your baby becomes jaundiced, you will notice the whites of his eyes and his skin look yellow. Your midwife might take some of his blood to check the level of jaundice. It is usually not much of a problem, and disappears of its own accord at around the tenth day but, very occasionally, certain babies might need some light therapy to help disperse it.

Affected babies are usually drowsy and therefore suckle weakly; they need to be woken up for feeds (perhaps every three hours during the day and every four hours at night). If you find that your baby keeps falling asleep rather than feeding, try taking some of his clothes off, so he is a little less comfortable, and put him back to the breast. Alternatively, during a feed you can withdraw the nipple (if you are not sore), massage his feet or stroke him under his chin when he stops sucking. You may also find it helps to wake him up if you change his nappy halfway through a feed, and then put him back to the second breast. Although all this sounds a little heartless, the reason is not only to give your baby the calories he needs, but to ensure that your milk supply is encouraged. When he recovers from the jaundice (and decides he is starving) you will then have enough milk to give him.

# VISITORS

You should be visited by a community midwife. How often and for how many days seems to depend on the area in which you live. This will be at least one new face, possibly several if the community midwives work as a team. They will check that your uterus is contracting down to its original size and inspect your stitches to ensure they are healing well. They will also weigh your baby and check his cord site as well as answering any questions you have. The community midwives are wonderfully calming and reassuring. They cannot guarantee to call at a particular time, however, so it is helpful to have someone else in the house to answer the door if you are sleeping or feeding.

Other visitors such as family and friends are easier to organise; give them times to call. The same principles apply as in the postnatal ward (see page 80): not too many at once and not for too long – it only takes a few minutes to see a new baby. There is an issue about small children visiting, as they frequently harbour viruses, which your baby doesn't need at the moment. Dissuade your family and friends from bringing round any of their children who have a cold and try, tactfully, to prevent any small child kissing (breathing all over!) your baby. This issue obviously needs very sensitive handling. Don't feel you have to leap around playing the ultra-competent hostess; visitors can sort themselves out and are probably pleased to be of practical help. You might even ask them to do some shopping for you.

**No visitor (or parent) should smoke in the house.**

At approximately six to seven days, a community midwife will prick your baby's heel to take a tiny amount of blood. This blood will be sent off so that it can be screened for various rare conditions which would need early treatment (you will be given a leaflet on this). About now you may also be visited by a health visitor (or sometimes a trained hearing screener) who will carry out a screening test for hearing problems.

# CHAPTER 10:

## Starting feeding

The first week is when you really get to grips with feeding. This is particularly important if you are breast-feeding; if you take the time to get it right now – particularly ensuring an adequate supply of milk – things will be considerably less fraught in a month's time when life hots up. Your priority is to make milk and for you and your baby to gain confidence in the whole process.

**Your most important task is to ensure that your baby has enough calories to put on weight.** If he has lost weight in his first few days, as many babies do, he may get back to birth weight by the end of this first week or even before, though the average baby will not do this until he is 10 days old.

## YOUR MILK 'COMING IN'

On day three or day four (occasionally a day or two later) your colostrum is replaced by milk. This is known as the milk 'coming in'. You will know when this happens, because far more milk is produced than colostrum, so your breasts will swell as the new milk distends them.

# PRIMARY ENGORGEMENT

In a few women, this swelling is so dramatic that their breasts become distended by up to three bra cup sizes so that they become enormous, tender and sometimes extremely painful. (Some women describe it as though they have been hit in the breasts with a cricket bat.) This is known as primary engorgement.

The over-distended breasts can also become so rounded that there is not enough nipple protruding for the baby to latch onto properly. This means that you have a double problem – too full a breast and too flat a nipple so your baby can't feed. Should this happen to you, do not despair. **It is a temporary phase and will pass within 48 hours** – you and your baby will both get through it. But while it lasts it can be pretty unpleasant.

If you are at home, try expressing milk by hand or, if this doesn't work, take off a small amount of milk with a pump so you are more comfortable. Electric or hand breast pumps can be bought from a chemist (although more expensive, most people find electric pumps easier and more comfortable). You will also need to take some painkillers – paracetamol is quite compatible with breast-feeding. If this doesn't work, take ibuprofen (Nurofen etc.). The amount of this in breast milk is too small to be harmful, even though some manufacturers say you shouldn't take it when breast-feeding. This is an unreasonably defensive instruction.

If you are still in hospital, tell the ward sister, who may also suggest a breast pump if things become desperate. Some hospitals are not keen on this as, in theory, a pump encourages the breasts to produce even more milk. However, if you are severely engorged, pumping off a small amount of milk *will not* make the engorgement worse.

Hopefully, taking a small amount of milk from the engorged breast will also sort out the flattened nipple problem, so your baby will be able to latch on properly and feed.

Your breasts must be well supported and you will be grateful that you had the foresight to buy a well-fitting maternity bra, even though you thought it looked ghastly at the time. Properly supported, your breasts will feel more comfortable (and less likely to develop stretch marks). It often helps to rest cold flannels on your engorged breasts, and when you put your bra back on, a traditional remedy is to place a fresh cold cabbage leaf (straight from the fridge) into each bra cup. There is something about cabbage leaves (the type is not important) which ensures they stay colder longer than almost anything else. Alternatively, you can buy chillable gel pads from a chemist.

# BREAST-FEEDING YOUR BABY – NOW WITH REAL MILK!

## Posture

Take the trouble to find a comfortable position for feeding. If you and your baby are comfortable, a feed is much more likely to go well. You are also going to be feeding your baby for several months, so if you get into good postural habits during these early days you will help prevent future shoulder and upper back problems.

It is important to **take your baby up to the breast, not your breast down to the baby.** This means raising him up to the right level by putting him on a pillow on your lap. It may help further if you put a foot on a stool in order to raise your thigh on the side he is feeding from. Traditional nursing chairs are intentionally low so that when you sit on them with your feet on the floor your thighs are automatically raised. All this stops you leaning forward to feed and thus straining your back.

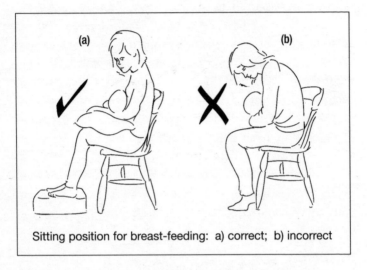

Sitting position for breast-feeding: a) correct; b) incorrect

While you are sitting in a chair to feed, get your bottom well back so the small of your back is supported by the chair. Drop your shoulders and relax when he starts to suckle.

## Getting your baby latched on at the correct angle

Firstly, lie your baby on the pillow on his side, close to your body, with his mouth close to your nipple. You may have to enlist the help of someone to work out this next bit:

1. Look at the direction your nipple is pointing (all nipples point in different directions).
2. Then take your baby to your breast with his face and mouth aligned to the nipple direction so that your nipple and most of the areola goes straight into his mouth.

3. The pillow may now need to be rearranged so it supports his head.

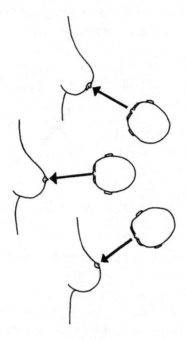

Then, a few things to consider:

- Hold your baby with your hand behind his shoulders and one finger supporting his head gently (see overleaf). **Don't cup his head in the palm of your hand and push him to your breast as he will panic, instinctively pull away and do anything rather than suckle.**
- When your baby is suckling, check that there is no puckering in the skin around the nipple. If there is, it means he is not properly aligned – go back to point 2. If the tiny breast ducts are kinking, the milk flow will be interrupted.
- Because he has to breathe through his nose, check this isn't obstructed by the rest of your breast.

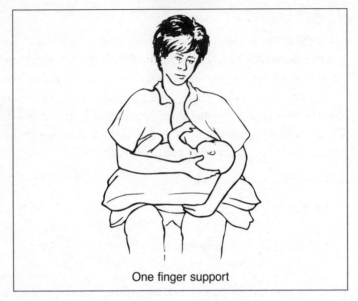

One finger support

If your nipples are shaped like teats, life is easy for both of you. If not, you may need to help your baby. If your nipple seems rather too flat, you can make the tip of your breast into the same shape as the open mouth of your baby by putting your thumb and index fingers at three o'clock and nine o'clock, just to the side of the areola (the brown area round the nipple). A common, but wrong, piece of advice is to tell you to put your fingers at 12 o'clock and six o'clock, which actually makes things more difficult for him.

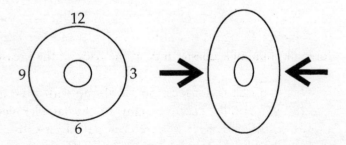

## One breast or two?

Some midwives have been taught that it is important for a breast to be completely emptied at a feed so that the baby gets the hindmilk from the back of the breast which contains rather more fat than the foremilk at the front. They will argue that this is more likely to happen if the baby feeds from only one breast at each feed.

This is mistaken on various counts:

- The physiology is wrong.
- The evidence does not support the practice over traditional feeding with two breasts per feed.
- It is irrelevant in any case.

Taking the last point first, it can be shown that babies regulate their own fat intake by their style of feeding. More importantly it has been repeatedly shown that it is **only the *volume* of milk taken, not the fat content, that has been shown to link to weight gain.**

Working back up the list, it has been shown that babies who fed from one breast at a feed grow no more rapidly than those fed from two breasts.

Then there is the question of the physiology. (Skip this if you want.)

Hindmilk is not some magic ingredient; it is simply that, during a feed, milk gradually increases in fat content the emptier a breast gets. Breasts *only* create what we call hindmilk, but some fat globules lag behind a little as the milk moves forwards towards the nipple and becomes foremilk; hindmilk doesn't lurk at the back of the breast forever.

When a breast is not fed from, it fills up with what is effectively foremilk, because many of the fat globules formed at the back have not yet been pulled forward as they would be by the baby sucking. The fuller the breast, the lower the fat content of the milk. Thus the breast that is not fed from at any one feed will contain less fat in its milk when the baby comes to it at the next feed.

The longer between feeds, the lower the fat content of breast milk. In other words, if a breast is not used at a feed it will fill with very low-fat milk. Any advantage in fat intake the baby obtained from the previous one-breast-only feed is cancelled out as the baby moves to the full, low-fat breast at the next feed.

This has been likened to running a hot tap. First there is cold water, then warmer, until hot. If you leave the tap off for a long time there will be a longer wait for hot water to come through whereas if you return to it fairly soon you won't have to wait so long.

Then there is the issue of making things easier for the baby to obtain a sufficient volume of milk (the key issue). Feeding from two breasts at each feed makes it easier for a baby to take milk because the let-down reflex affects both breasts meaning that the baby has two opportunities to suck easily and take more milk. Draining the last vestiges of milk from a virtually empty breast is hard going, and babies tend to fall asleep at this stage. Transferring to a full second breast is rewarding and almost certainly results in a higher volume intake.

So far, therefore, the lack of hard evidence for its benefit and an understanding of physiology indicate that there is no advantage in one-breast-only feeding. Our observations are that there seem to be some disadvantages, too:

- a higher rate of women developing mastitis (presumably from the breast being less frequently flushed through because of six-hour rather than three-hour intervals between use)
- more women complaining of insufficient milk at about seven weeks (using the second breast at the end of the first-breast feed nearly always resolves this!).

Most women have better success oft̲.
both breasts at each feed, starting the bab̲
moving on to the other when he seems to
enough – and indeed, this is what billions of n̲.
and babies have done historically. You should start v̲. ̲n
the breast that your baby finished on at his previous
feed. At the end of each feed, you could put a safety pin
in the bra strap of the second breast to remind you to
start with that one next feed time.

## How long?

This will largely depend on your baby (baby-led feeding)
but it is certainly not a good idea to keep him plugged on
for as long as possible (baby-led feeding within reason).

A baby who seems totally uninterested in feeding and
has to be coaxed to suckle will want (and need) to stay
on the breast for a longer period than a baby with a very
powerful suck. If a baby with a strong suck is left
suckling too long, he can readily produce sore nipples. It
is worth remembering that just because a baby constantly
wants to suckle at the breast, it doesn't necessarily mean
that he wants more milk. He may just like sucking.

As a guideline, let your baby feed from one breast until
he seems to have had enough – he either stops sucking
properly and/or falls asleep. This will usually be after 10
to 20 minutes. Then try to wind him, change his nappy
and offer him the second breast.

Provided that your baby suckles more or less
continuously (and you have enough milk), a total feed-
time should not take longer than around 45 minutes. A
baby takes most of the milk he needs in the first five
minutes when his suck is strongest, and new babies
cannot manage protracted periods of suckling.

## How often?

Please don't even think about routines at this stage! Your priorities are to get your milk supply established so you are producing the right amount for your baby. It takes time for your breasts and your baby (jointly) to establish enough milk production for each feed.

During their first week, most babies over 7 lb (3.2 kg) in weight will need to be fed around every three to three and a half hours during the day and every four hours at night. He will have one longer period between feeds – hopefully during the night. In the interests of ensuring a good milk supply, **he must have a minimum of six, usually seven feeds during a 24-hour period**; so, in this first week, do not leave him longer than six hours at night without feeding him. Small babies will need relatively more frequent feeds than heavier babies, and jaundiced babies (see page 105) may have to be woken every three hours until the jaundice subsides.

# COMMON BREAST-FEEDING PROBLEMS

Below are two common problems in the first week. If our first aid suggestions don't work, try reading *What to Expect When You're Breast-Feeding ... And What If You Can't?* by Clare Byam-Cook. She is a true expert on infant feeding.

## Sore nipples (or excruciatingly sore, even cracked, nipples)

This is, in our experience, the most common reason for giving up breast-feeding. Fair-skinned women and those who burn easily in the sun have nipples that are particularly vulnerable.

Poor latching-on is a well-recognised cause, as the baby has to suck for longer to get adequate colostrum or milk. We have also been struck by the escalating number of mothers with sore nipples since it has been fashionable to encourage mothers to allow their babies to suckle for protracted periods (sometimes hours!) in the first few days.

Sore nipples may progress to a cracked nipple, which is extraordinarily painful and can bleed so you see blood in the baby's mouth or, even worse, he may vomit dark blood (which will be yours, not his). Although this is alarming for you, it won't harm your baby.

This is a typical scenario:

- *Day one*
Your baby suckles for well over 15 minutes on each breast, but you don't mind because it is such a joyful experience and you have been told you are doing so well.

- *Day two*
Baby is still suckling for long periods; the joy is wearing off as your nipples are becoming quite tender.

- *Day three*
Your nipples are in agony and, if you are unlucky, also cracked and bleeding. You are, by now, at home, so you let your baby suckle for the shortest possible time and give him a 'top-up' bottle.

- *Day four*
Your milk comes in and you get primary engorgement (see page 110). Help! Now your breasts are so full it is hard for your baby to latch on and, in any case, he is

not that hungry (as he has had top-up bottles). The situation becomes even worse and everyone is distraught.

If things are so painful that you are having difficulty in feeding your baby try the following first aid until your nipples have healed:

- Take two paracetamol with water every four hours.
- Start each feed from the less painful nipple first (forget starting on alternating sides for the time being).
- Try using a nipple shield (bought from a chemist) for about five minutes at the start of a feed. A nipple shield can be a life-saver, but use it for emergencies only, as it tends to reduce your milk supply if used for too long. Only use a nipple shield once your milk has come through – a baby can't take colostrum via a shield.
- If things get too bad, use an electric breast pump. Pump the milk from the worst affected breast (pumping is not as painful as a baby sucking) while you carry on feeding with the other one if you can – at least until it packs up through over-use. Put the expressed (pumped) breast milk in a bottle for your baby then give it to him from the bottle.

Some people find creams helpful, but generally it is better to allow the nipple to dry by taking your bra off. A useful alternative is to put a breast-shell from the chemist into your bra to hold the material away from the nipple and allow air to circulate. What you don't want is your nipple wallowing in soggy breast pads.

## Your baby doesn't suck

This may be because you have an unusual nipple shape or your nipple is inverted. In such circumstances you need expert, individual attention from an experienced midwife or feeding counsellor to help your baby latch on. Occasionally, a baby has a very short frenulum under his tongue (tongue-tie), which makes it difficult or sometimes impossible for him to suck. This needs assessment by a paediatrician.

A baby with oral thrush (infection with candida) will have a sore mouth and may be in two minds about sucking. This is not a serious condition, but if you can see white patches inside his mouth you need to take him to your GP.

# BOTTLE-FEEDING

Try to feed your baby with your colostrum if you can. If not, most hospitals will suggest you start your baby on formula milk, often as early as on the first day, and show you how to feed him. Your breasts will still fill with milk. Although feasible, it is not common practice to give you any medication to 'dry the milk up'. Wear a well-fitting bra with the straps tightened and take painkillers if your breasts are very painful (see page 110). As you don't need to worry about your milk being baby-friendly you can concentrate on being mother-friendly and take whatever painkillers you like! It will take a few days for your breasts to get the message that they are not being required to produce any more milk, and the milk you have already made will be slowly reabsorbed.

The advantage of bottle-feeding is its sheer flexibility and the freedom it gives (one of you) to sleep through the night and go out during the day or evening. It is also easier to master; we cannot remember ever being rung by a mother having a crisis with bottle-feeding. Apart from the general principle of keeping the bottle equipment sterile, the only other likely complication is technical troubles with the teat, though these are now rare. It should deliver one drop a second when the bottle is held upside down.

You need not feed so frequently with a bottle, as formula milk takes longer than breast milk to digest. Most babies need to be fed around every three and a half hours and take more or less the amounts recommended on the packet.

You can warm a feed by putting the bottle in a jug of hot water. In spite of official guidance, many people use a microwave, but be very, very careful to shake the bottle well after heating, as it will have been warmed unevenly. Microwave ovens produce 'hot-spots' in milk that can burn unless they have been dispersed by vigorous shaking. Always check the temperature of the milk by allowing a few drops to fall on the inside of your wrist before offering the bottle to the baby. You are checking that it is not too hot – some babies are quite happy with cold milk and it makes no nutritional difference.

It is relatively easy to overfeed a bottle-fed baby, especially in the first few days, not so much because of too much milk, but because the feed has been made up with too much powder. Measure the quantities carefully, and don't insist he finishes the bottle. There isn't as much difference between different milks as you might think. A midwife or health visitor can advise you, but don't get into soya without the supervision of your GP or paediatrician, because its nutritional balance is different.

# CHAPTER 11:

## Ten days to three weeks old

With any luck your baby will still be relatively quiet for the next week or so. This period, up to when your baby is three weeks old, is a time for you to continue concentrating on recovering physically from labour and birth, and for you, your husband and your baby to get to know each other. Live your life in the slow lane. If you are breast-feeding, it is also the time to continue to lay the foundations for a good milk supply. Mature milk (full of calories) takes up to two weeks to come in. Long-term success in breast-feeding pivots on this early period. You need rest, and your breasts need regular suckling from your baby – as mentioned, a minimum of six feeds (usually seven) in a 24-hour period. All this will be accomplished most successfully if you remain quietly at home. Nipping into the office followed by a quick dash round the supermarket will neither help your stitch-line to heal nor your milk supply to flourish.

If your husband has only had a few days off to see you and your baby back home, he will now have gone back to work. He might hand over to your mother, who could move in if that is what suits you both. Having someone at home (or visiting daily) is often helpful in ensuring you eat proper meals; this means breakfast, a decent lunch (not a diet yoghurt and a packet of crisps) and supper.

When he is back at work, he should certainly not expect you to be bouncing around, conjuring up tasty evening meals or entertaining friends for supper. He needs to come home promptly and avoid the temptation to linger with his mates. You (and his baby) come first.

Should your husband have been lucky enough to negotiate more extended paternity leave, his job is to help you to stay in the slow lane. He should take on some housework, the shopping and the general organisation of household chores. This means planning meals and their preparation in advance, for example, rather than hovering around looking for an opportunity to be useful or slumping in front of the television. It is possible that he may need some guidance – for example, your evening meal needs to be earlier than he might think. Not many women at this stage are going to want to be hanging around for a four-course gourmet dinner at 9.30pm.

Much (or all!) of your waking day is going to be spent feeding, changing, washing and comforting your baby. You will by now be feeling slightly less dazed and a little more capable, but take things more slowly than you would usually as you still won't feel very organised. It is really important that you get as much sleep as you can, which means a day-time nap is a priority. (And this is exactly what new mothers don't do!) If you have someone at home with you, it's clearly their role to take your baby for an hour or two in the afternoon so you can go to bed. Even if you don't feel like going to sleep, have an afternoon rest.

Your lochia will now be lessening but if you pass any large clots keep them, if possible, to show your health visitor.

In theory, you will want to discard your night-gear and get into tracksuit bottoms or similar, but you are likely to find it takes you half the day to get dressed. Unhappily, unless you are very lucky, most of your ordinary clothes will not yet fit. Do not worry about this or decide to go on a diet at this stage – it is too early to deal with the problem of a few extra pounds now. Incidentally, if you are breast-feeding you may notice that you are continually hungry and crave sweet things. Listen to your body and eat what you feel like, so long as you maintain a reasonably balanced diet.

## TUMMY MUSCLES AND BACKACHE

You may notice to your dismay that you still look pregnant, especially if you have had a Caesarean section. Unless you are very lucky, your abdominal muscles will be stretched and weak. At this stage, **concentrate on holding your lower tummy muscles in while you are standing and walking.** This will restore the elasticity of the muscles, which is necessary before you begin active tummy exercises. The abdominal muscles are responsible for protecting your lower back – and if you are suffering from low backache it is likely to be due to weak tummy muscles rather than weak back muscles. This is especially relevant if you had a Caesarean section.

While you are around the house, don't cover up a pot belly with a baggy sweater so that you forget about it – wear something that continually reminds you to hold your tummy in.

# POSTNATAL EXERCISES

There are three things that are more important than any exercises:

- Getting into the habit of holding your tummy in when you are standing and walking (as above).
- Being very careful to bend your knees and keep your lower back straight when lifting anything.
- Making sure your baby's changing table is the same height as your waist.

Realistically, there are very few newly-delivered mothers that will have the time or energy to turn on a DVD and tackle half an hour of postnatal exercises and, in any case, these are best done under the eye of a teacher/trainer. If you are lucky, your hospital, health centre or local NCT might run classes but check out what is involved. Prancing around in a leotard is simply not on, though Pilates classes are good news. Otherwise, when your baby is six weeks old, you may find your local gym has a specialist postnatal or Pilates class. Incidentally, no exercise that you do should give you low backache.

Nevertheless, if you have the time and inclination, the following two basic exercises can be started as soon as you like and will begin to help your tummy muscles recover.

Lying on the floor with a pillow under your head:

1. *Basic pelvic tilt and pelvic floor*
With knees bent, flatten the small of your back against the floor and relax. Now flatten your back again, pull up your pelvic floor, then relax your pelvic floor and relax your back. Do this five times.

2. *Tummy tightening*

Lie on your side with your knees bent. Put your hand on your lower tummy. Take a deep breath in. Then, breathing out, pull your tummy away from your hand towards your back. Keep your tummy drawn in for a slow count of 10 while breathing normally. Do this five times. Once you have mastered this, you can pull your tummy in without using your hand as a guide and in any position (such as feeding while sitting).

# PELVIC FLOOR

Now is the time to focus on your pelvic floor and whether you are, in fact, contracting the muscles properly. To do this, tighten the following simultaneously:

- the anal sphincter muscles – as though you need to stop passing wind
- the opening of the vagina – as though you are trying to stop a tampon falling out
- the urethra area – imagining you have a full bladder but the loo is engaged.

## Fast contraction

Hold the contraction for a count of two. Then relax the muscles, and you should feel a slight 'drop' between your legs as the muscles return to their former position. If you can feel this then you have successfully contracted the pelvic floor muscles. Neither your buttock muscles nor your eyebrows should be working at the same time, nor should you hold your breath! This is a fast contraction – or 'flick' – which will keep the muscles toned.

## Sustained (slow) contraction

This does more than restore tone; it will actually strengthen the pelvic floor muscles so needs to be added to the quick flicks. Concentrating on the vagina, squeeze and lift the pelvic floor as powerfully as possible and hold the contraction for as long as you can, breathing normally. Try initially to sustain it for a slow count of six. If this presents no problem, and the muscle fibres haven't started to relax before you want them to, try sustaining the contraction for a count of 10. A reasonable goal will be to sustain a contraction for a slow count of around 30 by the time your baby is about six months (three months if you had a Caesarean).

A good way to remember is to do them while you are feeding – 10 contractions (five fast, five slow) for each breast or, if you are bottle-feeding, 10 contractions for the first 25 ml and 10 contractions for the last 25 ml. At this stage you will find that your buttock and/or your abdominal muscles will want to contract at the same time, so you need to concentrate on isolating the pelvic floor muscles. This means that when you do a pelvic floor contraction no other muscle should move! (Physiotherapist mothers will know that the transversus abdominis will contract simultaneously but ordinary mortals won't be aware of this.) Occasionally, you may want to check if you can stop peeing in midstream – eventually you will be able to stop the flow of urine, but for the time being, be content if you can just slow it.

# KEEPING A FOOT IN THE OUTSIDE WORLD

Plan no more than one social activity a day. A friend for coffee and your mother-in-law for tea may well be too much.

Friends who haven't had babies can be a bit of a problem; see only a few of them. As they have not experienced primary maternal preoccupation themselves, they do not realise that you are in your own time capsule. They may not understand why you hadn't noticed that World War III broke out yesterday, or why you don't care if it has. They will go home saying to their friends, 'Oh my God, we've lost her. Can't think of anything but the baby. Talk about vague. She's completely knocked off.'

If you went to an antenatal class you might like to check your emails or make a few phone calls to other class members to see if they have had their babies yet. You won't feel quite so much on your own if you can chat to other new mothers about how things have been and how things are, but don't get competitive about your baby's feeding and sleeping patterns. After the first week at home, the community midwife hands over to the health visitor, who will probably ring to fix a visit and get to know both you and your baby. She will tell you where your local child health clinic is (it might be at your GP's surgery) and which day to take your baby to be weighed there every week or two, at least for the first few months.

If you haven't been given a Child Health Record in hospital, the health visitor will give you one. This is a book that is kept by you and contains entries from any healthcare professionals who have dealings with your baby. It is your baby's medical record and the argument is that it is less likely to be lost if you keep it than if it is consigned to the mercy of a medical records department.

Depending on the season and the outside temperature, aim for a trip outdoors with the baby when you can face it (this can seem a major hurdle). Discover precisely how to get to the child health clinic, or go and register the baby at the local register office. If you and your baby's father are not married you both have to go in person, so this will involve him taking some (more) time off work.

At some stage, before your baby starts to get restless in the evenings (which begins at about three weeks), see if you can get someone (your mother?) to look after your baby while you and your husband try and get out of the house for a quick meal or a drink and some time together. You are not only a mother: you are still a wife, confidante, best friend and lover. But don't let him even contemplate sex yet – you certainly won't.

# YOUR BABY

Keep cuddling your baby (of course!). Don't let him go more than four hours between feeds during the day (count from the start of a feed): you may need to wake him for a feed if necessary. Otherwise don't keep prodding and fiddling with him when he is resting – he needs to sleep as much as he can. Talk to him and enjoy him when he is alert, but don't be too impatient to have major fun with him; he needs a quiet couple of weeks to adapt to the outside world. Your voice, your face and your smell is all the stimulation he needs at this stage. The baby gym and rattles can wait.

Have confidence in feeling you don't have to try too hard. Remember that you do not have to try to be a super-mother – simply being there for him and remaining sensitive to his needs is entirely adequate. Trying to do more is likely to unsettle everyone. Keep him swaddled and lying on his back. He will still have a floppy head which needs support when you pick him up, and this will continue to be the case for another few weeks.

# FEEDING

There is only one thing that really matters – your baby should be starting to put on weight. Although it is usual for babies to lose up to 10 per cent of their birth weight in the first few days, he should now (at 10 days to two weeks) be back to his birth weight. **If he has not regained his birth weight, this needs attention,** no matter who tells you it's OK because you are breast-feeding. It is absolutely *not* OK for a baby to fail to put on weight at this stage, irrespective of whether he is breast-fed or not. In the early weeks, babies need an adequate quantity (indicated by weight gain) of fats and amino acids for their brain development.

If you are breast-feeding, you and your baby should be settling into a feeding rhythm that suits you both, whereas if you are bottle-feeding, you will probably have got it licked. With any luck you will be feeling much more relaxed about feeding times. Most babies will be feeding roughly every three hours during the day and taking six to eight feeds in a 24-hour period. Please don't get hung up on a four-hourly routine.

In order to take a good feed your baby needs to be:
- rested enough (so the comforting action of sucking doesn't send him to sleep before he has finished)
- hungry enough (at least two hours since the beginning of the previous feed so you don't encourage a habit of snacking).

So-called demand feeding does not mean whipping out a breast at every whimper from your baby. It means feeding your baby when he is genuinely hungry, rather than making him wait the next 17 minutes according to some rigid routine.

## Not enough breast milk?

This has nothing to do with breast size. As a first step, do not resort to supplementary bottles, unless your baby is really hungry. If you are feeding from one breast at each feed, start to offer him the second breast as well. If you are feeding from two breasts, try offering more frequent feeds on the basis that the more your breasts are emptied, the more milk they will produce. You will need to offer at least two extra feeds in a 24-hour period, so you will probably have to wake your baby to feed him.

## Supply and demand

It may help to remember that your breasts will produce as much milk as is removed from them. Effectively they have a memory for how much milk was taken from them – and will re-fill accordingly. If your breasts are not producing enough (your baby doesn't settle after a feed and is not putting on enough weight), feed your baby more often so that more milk is taken. More milk will then be produced. If a hungry baby is given a supplementary bottle (or if he is given a bottle at night), he will be less hungry and empty the breasts less well at his next feed – and so on. If your baby is given a top-up bottle, your breasts have no way of knowing that they haven't produced enough milk, so won't realise that they need to produce more.

## Vomiting

You may have a baby who throws up. Roughly speaking, there are six patterns to this:

1. Some babies, mainly those that are breast-fed, seem greedy and positively gulp down their feed, which then bounces back.

2. Although a baby has to suck to obtain milk from a bottle, some breasts produce a flow of milk that literally spurts and overwhelms a small baby's capacity to deal with it.

3. Other babies – most often baby girls – are just sicky babies and 'posset' small quantities of milk every time they are picked up. It drives their mothers to distraction yet there is absolutely nothing to worry about, apart from the smell that lingers on your clothes. After a while you get used to carrying around a muslin square ('puke rag') with you and putting it on anyone's shoulder if they are going to hold the baby. The amount they bring up always looks more than it actually is, and it is extremely unlikely that the baby will starve. Mothers frequently worry about this type of baby vomiting, but if the baby is putting on weight it is very unlikely there is anything seriously wrong. This type of vomiting will stop at about the time the baby starts to crawl – which unfortunately doesn't start until a baby is about seven months.

4. If your baby catches a cold he may vomit because he is swallowing mucus. (See 'Colds' overleaf.)

5. A very few babies, mainly boys, develop projectile vomiting, which means that they can eject a stream of vomit for nearly a metre. Such vomiting usually interferes with the baby's weight gain, but in any case you should consult your GP sooner rather than later as the cause may be pyloric stenosis. This is an uncommon physical condition which prevents the stomach from emptying properly, and it will need treatment.

6. Vomiting after *every* feed may indicate reflux (see page 214).

# COLDS

A baby catches a cold because of a virus, not because he has an incompetent mother who left him in a draught or who took him for a walk (without dressing him properly) and got caught in the rain. Colds are a problem before the age of six weeks because a tiny baby finds it difficult to breathe through his mouth. This is frightening for the parents. He also finds feeding with a blocked-up nose difficult and quickly tires. Yet babies must keep up their fluid intake, particularly if they have a temperature. You can temporarily kiss goodbye any pattern of feeding which may have been emerging, because you might have to feed every two hours. Keep your baby in the same room as you and don't let him overheat. A room humidifier will help keep his nose unblocked and enable him to breathe more easily. Call your GP if he has a temperature, if his snot turns green, if he goes off his food, or if you are simply worried.

# CHAPTER 12:

## Three to six weeks old

At two to three weeks many babies start to come out of the rather dozy ('good') state they have been in up to now. In particular they come to life in the evenings, often quite noisily. Their previously quiet demeanour has helped to shield them from too much stimulation too early but now they're getting up for it (even if you aren't). As they warm up, their individual personality or temperament becomes more clearly defined (you might like to look at Chapter 16). It is now that your baby begins to take an active interest in the world around him. His eyes seek out complex patterns but your face is still the most fascinating thing as far as he is concerned.

### YOU

Any manic buzz will have worn off and it is likely that you are now feeling somewhat drained. Nevertheless, you have to rise to the occasion and cope with an increasingly demanding baby. If you have been lucky enough to have someone staying in your house in order to help you, they will probably leave at some stage in these three weeks.

You will be on your own for much of the time, possibly with a crisis of confidence. Don't set yourself too high a standard; your task is to survive. Hang on in there; it gets better in time.

For most of the day now you will be up in day clothes and pottering around. The days change little but you can expect the evenings to become a strain. From three weeks on, comforting your baby in the evening burns up a great deal of time. You will find yourself developing new expertise in pacing up and down, jiggling the baby and singing softly into his ear. Your husband gets used to coming home to the sound of a grizzling baby, and you both get used to having the baby with you at supper.

You will not yet be physically perfect! Your lochia will have started to tail off and turn progressively browner. It will stop at about five weeks. Meanwhile, if you have had dissolvable stitches, you may find what look like little worms on your pad as they break up and come away. Incidentally, it is wise to carry on using a pad/pantyliner even if you feel up to using a tampon because of the slight risk of infection ascending into the womb and the site where the placenta was attached.

## Your pelvic floor

Continue your pelvic floor exercises – this is a priority. You should still be aiming for 50 contractions a day in groups of five plus five, and hopefully will have programmed yourself to do them while feeding. You should find by now that you are better at slowing (or even stopping) the flow of urine in midstream – but only check this occasionally.

Don't despair if, in spite of masses of pelvic floor exercises, your muscles don't seem to respond very well. It is still early days and, if you had a long or difficult second stage of labour, especially with forceps, it is going to take longer for your pelvic floor muscles to recover.

Most women will not be thinking of sex yet, except with apprehension. If you have already had sex, that's great. You won't have done any damage (but unless you were careful to take precautions you may now be pregnant again!).

# FEEDING

As previously mentioned, most breast-fed babies will need at least six or seven feeds a day. You may be fortunate and notice a pattern emerging. If your baby is feeding well, there should be a general impression of three- to four-hourly feeds during the day, rather chaotic feeding throughout the evening and the occasional unbroken spell of six hours during the night. It is, however, quite normal for babies not to show signs of any such pattern. Be patient – it is still too early to impose routines. A bottle-fed baby will probably be taking six feeds a day.

If a breast-fed baby isn't settling after a feed, try giving him another feed during the day. Milk volumes increase and then stabilise at about four weeks so it is very important to lay down a secure foundation of adequate milk intake before attempting to encourage any feeding pattern. **You mustn't impose any feeding routines until you know your milk supply is up to your baby's requirements** (which you can only tell if he is putting on the right amount of weight).

Start weekly visits to your local clinic to get your baby weighed. He should gain an average of approximately 7 oz (200 g) a week or 15 oz (450 g) a fortnight. It is important to know that his weight gain is good enough when you are trying to work out why he may be crying (see page 211). You don't need to buy scales for weighing him daily at home; weekly weighing gives a better overall view.

## Introducing your baby to a teat

There is a real problem with many breast-fed babies refusing to take a bottle (of anything). This causes their mothers enormous distress and exasperation later on.

If you are breast-feeding, start getting your baby used to an occasional bottle during the day so that he adds the skill of teat-sucking to his competence at nipple-sucking. Some professionals think that introducing a breast-fed baby to a bottle will cause him 'nipple–teat confusion' and throw up their hands in horror. Certainly it often takes a baby a few minutes to adapt to a switch between nipple and teat (or vice versa) or from one sort of teat to another (from Avent to Playtex, for example). This is not in any way a major issue, is unlikely to cause any breast-feeding problems and indeed is an opportunity for your clever baby to learn a new skill. The concept of nipple-teat confusion as a problem seems to have arisen because a baby may reject the nipple of a breast that isn't producing enough milk and understandably prefer a teat that does.

Your baby's ability to take a bottle frees you up. This extends beyond the possible night-time advantages of eventually allowing your husband to bail you out in the wee small hours. If your baby will take only from the breast, your mobility during the day will be severely constrained, something which does not matter now but is likely to be important in a few months' time – even if you are not planning to return to work.

You can put breast milk into the bottle or, if he will take it, previously-boiled water. Of course, if you want to start to transfer to bottle-feeding you will use formula. Remember that breast-fed babies are used to taking their milk at a constant body temperature (quite warm), which means you may have better success with whatever is in the bottle if it is slightly warmer than you would like to drink it yourself.

The point is to get him used to taking a teat every day, not to provide nutrition but to get him used to sucking on a teat rather than a nipple. If he has been using a dummy you will probably find he takes to a bottle more easily.

Some women find that they leak milk from the breast that the baby is not feeding from, which removes the need to express. If you are one of these mothers, buy something called a breast-shell (not shield) from the chemist. This is a flat plastic cup that you sterilise and then put between your bra and nipple so it collects the leaking milk. Transfer this milk into a small custom-made plastic bag (also from the chemist) and then immediately into the freezer.

## Expressing breast milk

If you find you don't leak milk, you can express it. Some (but frankly, very few) mothers find they can express milk by hand, but most find an electric pump is the most comfortable and efficient method.

Even so, expressing milk isn't as straightforward as it sounds, as you have to work out when you are going to do it. Obviously you don't want to pump enthusiastically before a feed, as there won't be enough milk left in your breasts for your baby. Pumping between feeds means that you will seem to do little else during the day but bare your breasts. This leaves the option of pumping at the end of a feed, when most of – if not all – your milk will now be inside your baby. However, this third method is often the easiest. If you regularly pump off 25 ml or so at the end of a feed, you will have the added bonus of boosting your milk supply. These small amounts of milk can be frozen as described above.

You can then defrost enough bags to give him 30–50 ml in a bottle before one of his usual breast-feeds, or indeed, enough to replace an occasional whole feed. This won't upset his feed or your milk supply. (And you will also have a whole supply of breast milk in the freezer in case of an emergency.) The purpose of all this is to ensure he learns – and continues to remember – how to take fluid from a teat as well as from a nipple. It is in your interests to continue giving him milk or formula via a teat every day so he doesn't lose this skill.

Breast milk can be kept:
- in a freezer for up to three months
- in the fridge for up to 24 hours
- at room temperature for up to four hours (convenient for travelling), though not residual dregs from a previous feed.

## Mastitis

If you are breast-feeding you may be unlucky and notice a hard, slightly tender lump, possibly with a red patch or streak over it, developing in one of your breasts. This is almost certainly because a milk duct inside your breast has become blocked, causing milk behind the blockage to seep out into the breast tissue, which then becomes swollen and inflamed (mastitis).

This creates a fertile breeding ground for bacteria if these enter the area from the blood stream or through a badly cracked nipple, and a bacterial infection very commonly follows. You start to develop a temperature and feel as though you have 'flu – though if you are very sleep-deprived and already feeling like death, you may not notice these symptoms very much.

Unless treated promptly, the bacterial infection can lead to a breast abscess, which is a serious complication and will probably mean admission to hospital.

If you catch the blockage before bacterial infection has set in, you will have a tender, red lump but not a temperature (take it yourself), and you won't feel ill. You can try to unblock the duct yourself but make a prompt appointment to see your GP in any case as bacterial infections can develop very quickly (it is always Friday when these things happen).

It may be possible to unblock the duct if you turn your baby round to face the other way for a feed (his legs under your armpit rather than resting on your lap). This is called the 'football' hold, because it is how players hold an American football or a rugby ball when they're running with it (see overleaf). The different position of the baby alters the pattern of suction on the breast ducts. Then, while he is sucking, stroke downwards over the lump with your fingers or a large, wide-toothed comb. Take a hot bath and carry out the same stroking action, or use a pump, alternating this with a hot flannel applied to the affected breast. Over the next few days, keep taking your temperature in order to detect any bacterial infection at the earliest possible stage.

If your GP does diagnose an infection, treatment is urgent; antibiotics are required to kill the bacteria and prevent an abscess forming. Get these from a chemist promptly and down your throat as soon as possible.

**Even if your GP thinks that things are only at the stage of a blocked duct, ask for a prescription to have in hand so you can get some antibiotics quickly if the**

The 'football' hold

**signs of infection (a temperature and feeling ill) develop.** You don't want to find yourself trailing back to the surgery, possibly within hours, feeling awful and with a baby in tow, simply to be told that you now need a prescription.

Antibiotics work within 48 hours, so if the lump and your temperature have not begun to subside by then, contact your doctor again. (It will now be Sunday evening!) You should continue to breast-feed. Contrary to popular belief, neither the antibiotics nor the infection in the breast tissue will harm the baby, and his feeding will keep the breast drained. Only if your doctor tells you that you have an actual abscess will you need to stop feeding.

Bear in mind that mastitis may recur; some women are unlucky enough to have ducts that keep blocking.

# YOUR BABY

Day by day he is becoming physically more robust and noticeably bigger. His face may have broken out in unattractive spots, which should be ignored. They will go after a week or two. You may be concerned that he does not have a dirty nappy every day but breast-fed babies often don't. **A baby is not constipated unless his stools are hard.**

## Evening fretting

Between about three and 12 weeks of age, nine out of 10 babies will fret, grizzle or be otherwise grumpy and unsettled in the evening. This is often late evening, after six o'clock, and continues until 11 o'clock or later. This demanding light crying, which lessens briefly when you pick the baby up and soothe him, but returns when you put him down again, can follow a perfectly settled day. It is not just the appearance of your husband returning from work that triggers it; it happens on weekend evenings, too. Both you and your husband become adept at eating with one hand (baby in the other). In a few weeks' time you may wonder if you will ever again be able to have supper without your baby constantly present like Banquo's ghost. Don't panic – it is a temporary stage. Most babies are settling down to sleep before your supper (and remaining there) by three months.

It is possible that your baby is hungry, as the supply of some mothers' breast milk may be relatively low in the evenings, though it won't be 'thin' or 'weak' as is sometimes asserted. A hungry baby, however, will continue to cry when you pick him up. Obviously it is sensible to offer a fretful baby a feed if you think he is hungry, but remember that an unsettled baby will suck for comfort as well, so you can be misled as to why he was crying. You will know whether he is truly hungry by seeing if he does, in fact, take a full feed. Most babies who fret in the evening cannot settle themselves and seem to be windy, uncomfortable and over-tired rather than hungry. As they cry, babies can inadvertently suck air into their stomach and this results in, or worsens, wind problems.

Many babies need help to learn how to soothe themselves if uncomfortable or tired, and this is the reason why evening fretting is such a common problem. This is the time when everyone wants the baby to go to sleep but he does not yet know how to do it, especially if he is in discomfort because he is distended with wind. You know he must be tired, but he cannot get himself to sleep. After a bit his parents think it's actually that he won't (rather than can't) shut up and fall asleep, and it seems to them like a battle of wills or a behaviour problem that needs stern action. They get exasperated and this unsettles him further. The fretting is thus a combination of his inability to settle himself and his response to your (understandable) impatience.

The first thing to try is swaddling him (see page 91). This provides him with a sense of being contained and restrains his flailing limbs. Once swaddled, if you have a flat bouncing cradle it is worth trying to lie him in that while rocking him rhythmically and quite quickly – about two bouncelets per second. If this quietens him, you can both take it in turns to rock the chair as you try to eat supper. Alternatively, some babies stop crying and settle if they are placed on their tummy on a pillow on your lap, while you gently (and again rhythmically) pat their back.

Usually, the only answer for a fretting baby is to go along with it rather than spending the entire evening trying to settle him in his crib or cot. Pick him up, and place him along your forearm as shown below and pace (walk slowly up and down your hall or around your sitting room). The rhythm of steady walking provides a regular jiggle which is inherently soothing. Your free hand can hold his dummy in place. This method is better for your back than using an over-the-shoulder carrying technique, because you are less likely to slop into a pregnancy posture with resultant backache.

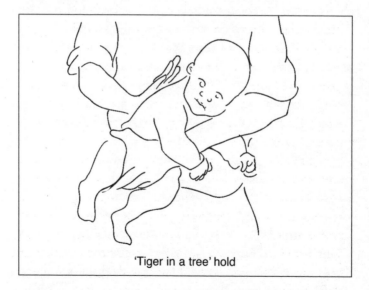

'Tiger in a tree' hold

**Your basic task is to be there for your baby and continue your efforts to soothe him, not to find the elusive remedy for his crying and certainly not to stimulate or distract him out of it.** If it is the case (as is sometimes said) that anxious mothers communicate their anxiety to their babies, then it is probably because they become too impatient to do anything soothing for long enough. If they anxiously keep trying different tactics – give him a feed, try to wind him, put him down, pick him up, bounce him, sing to him – but nothing is carried out for long enough, then he will get irritable or anxious, not being satisfied by any manoeuvre and not knowing what is coming next.

## Colic

A small number of babies (perhaps one in 20) will develop colic (see also Chapter 17) at about the third week of their lives. This is really a severe form of evening fretting and produces explosive outbursts of crying every evening that are severe, protracted and unresponsive to soothing. The baby draws his knees up to his chest, screams and gives every impression of being racked by spasms of tummy pain. Matters only subside after several hours. The whole problem disappears magically between 10 to 14 weeks (which is why it is sometimes called three-month colic).

A considerable amount of nonsense has been written about colic. Some professionals who should know better deny its existence and don't seem to have enough experience to tell the difference between colic and evening fretting (and certainly many people use the term 'colic' as a descriptive term for any evening crying). Others say that it is caused by maternal anxiety communicated to the child. Many mothers with colicky babies are indeed anxious, but this is much more likely to be effect rather than cause. More recently, a view has been expressed that colic is 'developmental' – in other words, that all babies do it at this age (yet they don't).

One problem is that no one has ever demonstrated the underlying cause of colic. It looks to an observer like the sort of pain produced by spasm of part of the intestines, and some affected babies were helped by medicines which relieved gut spasm. However, these were not helpful in all cases (and are no longer considered safe).

Perhaps because of this, numerous theories abound and this is another area in which you will hear conflicting advice from all quarters rather than an offer of respite care, which would be more to the point. Once again, everyone is an expert when it comes to the persistently crying baby. It is party-time for mother-blamers. Yet if anyone really knew the answer, they would be rich beyond their dreams. A favourite suggestion is that it is something that a breast-feeding mother has been eating – dairy products and salad (of all things) often seem to be blamed. Although a few new babies have persistent discomfort if their mothers eat a great deal of garlic, highly spiced foods or lots of citrus fruit, we have never ever seen a convincing case of three-month evening colic result from a mother's diet. As the colic is confined to the evenings it is rather hard to see why the baby should only be intolerant of the dietary irritant then. As far as the baby's diet is concerned, milk intolerance is rare and similarly will not cause problems specifically in the evening. As with any time-limited condition, a large number of treatments for colic (cranial osteopathy, baby massage, etc.) appear to 'work' at about 10 to 14 weeks of age.

Essentially, surviving colic requires the same strategy as coping with evening fretting. It is just that you have to carry it out under much more stressful conditions and share the load. (See page 216 for more on colic.) Remember that both evening fretting and colic are temporary, and both will pass by the time your baby is between 10 and 14 weeks. Eventually, you will find that you will be able to put him down for the night approximately five minutes earlier every night. It might be worth writing down the exact time he goes down for the night every evening, so you are reassured that things are actually getting better week by week.

## Reflux

Gastro-oesophageal reflux is a completely different problem from wind and colic and is often misdiagnosed. A baby with reflux will cry nearly all the time – day and night, especially during and after feeds because he is a truly distressed baby. He needs to see a doctor, preferably a paediatrician. (See page 214 for more on reflux).

# TALKING TO YOUR BABY

Babies love to be talked to and respond to it with increasing excitement as they get older. Talking to your baby helps his development as well as being fun in its own right. In the first place it helps build his language development, even before he can understand the words you use. He learns to associate your varying facial expressions with the different sounds of your voice. He learns the rhythms and sounds of the language you use.

Most importantly, he learns the art of turn-taking. This probably started even earlier when you began to feed him. Babies suck in bursts, so he would suck for a bit and then stop. You would jiggle the nipple in his mouth and he would get going again. Without thinking about it, you and he established a pattern of give-and-take. This is fundamental for learning how to talk with other people –

speaking and listening in turn. It is an experience that carries on through the way you talk to him even before he can reply. You find that you and he begin to mesh. You do something and he, in turn, responds. Or, indeed, the other way around. He does something and watches you respond. And then he responds to your response.

One of the most obvious things about adults and babies is the extent to which adults imitate babies (rather than vice versa, which is what everyone thinks). This is very obvious when babies start to talk but actually starts even before they begin to babble. Adults, especially mothers, imitate their baby's facial expressions. By doing so they reflect the baby's feelings back to him. The mother's face, already the most fascinating thing in his visual world, becomes a mirror for the baby. He sees his feelings copied in her face. In fact, if a mother keeps a still, unresponsive face, her baby becomes distressed.

At about six weeks, babies develop an infectious social smile. They begin to smile radiantly when someone looks at them face-to-face. It is a real social encounter. People will say, 'Have you got a smile out of him yet?' But it is more than that. If he smiles at you, you will smile back. You will imitate him. In fact, you don't have to smile at him to get a smile, but he will get one out of you all right! At first, a baby only needs to see a pair of eyes in a face to make him smile but as the weeks pass, it takes more to do so. At about 12 weeks he needs to see a face that talks before he smiles at it. Speech and smiling are thus closely linked in development. Talking to each other is a social activity. It is as if he is encouraging you to talk to him by rewarding you with a smile. And he plainly enjoys it. His smile gets broader and he wriggles with pleasure as you talk to him.

The power of a baby to engage other people in talking to him is demonstrated by the way in which he seems to encourage adults to use a special form of speech when talking to him. Sometimes called 'motherese', it is high-pitched, musical, repetitive, full of expression, is accompanied by much face-pulling, and occurs in all cultures. Mothers (and fathers) who use it bend over or pick the baby up so that their face is about a foot away from the baby's face. This is the distance at which small babies can focus their eyes most easily, but adults seem to know this intuitively. They then launch into short bursts of 'Who's a pretty, bitty, little baby then?' and the like. It works brilliantly; babies love it. They enjoy adults directing high-pitched, rhythmic, expressive, questioning speech to them. There is absolutely no point in trying to do anything more complicated. It's what they like.

You may hear 'motherese' criticised for being immature and ungrammatical. It is, of course, but it doesn't matter in the slightest. The point of it is that it is a communication, not a model of how to speak properly. At this stage communication is what counts. Simply reading leaders from *The Times* to your baby will do nothing for his language development. Responding to his facial expressions with some affectionate silly talk in 'motherese' is actually the best thing you can do. It is not trivial.

The current interest in baby signing (teaching a baby to use particular communicative gestures) is welcome, because it is an extension of what babies do in any case and gives parents and babies something specific to do together. In one study, babies who were taught to sign by their mothers did rather well developmentally compared to other babies. But the key scientific question is whether the other babies had the same amount of time together with their mothers, and that wasn't clear. Signing with your baby is good fun but mustn't replace talking to your baby, of course; they should co-exist. As things stand, there isn't enough evidence to say that it is important or how much you should do.

Incidentally, if you have a bilingual household, don't worry about using both languages when talking to your baby. Children from bilingual families do not have slower speech and language development, though their vocabulary in each language will be a little smaller than usual. Once again it's communication that is important, rather than the words you use.

# PART FOUR:

## Six Weeks Onwards

# CHAPTER 13:

## Six to 12 weeks old

By six weeks you find yourself left, quite literally, holding the baby. It may dawn on you that bringing up your baby is one of the most challenging things you will ever have to do, but you will be nudging towards normality and feeling more at ease with yourself as a mother. Your baby will start to smile broadly, and the emotional impact on you will be wonderful.

Evenings may still be tricky and hurdles like the return to work and sex loom ominously. The family show must be kept on the road but you simply need to continue with good-enough parenting, not feeling you have to try too hard to be perfect.

## YOUR SIX-WEEK CHECK

At six to eight weeks after the birth, you will have a check-up. This is not an indication that you should now be back to normal as you won't be. In fact, you are quite likely to still feel pretty sleep-deprived and in need of an afternoon nap, now (hopefully) well-established.

The check-up is a straightforward process and can be undertaken by your GP or your obstetrician, but you should be prepared for an internal examination. The purpose of this is to ensure that your uterus is shrinking down and in the right place, that your cervix is satisfactory, that you are not still bleeding and your stitches have healed. At the end of the examination you will be asked about contraception.

# SEX AND RELATIONSHIPS

Until they have had a reassurance that all is anatomically present and correct down below, most women feel very nervous about resuming sexual activity. Even when the six-week check has given them a confirmation that sex is mechanically possible, the vast majority will find themselves devoid of any libido whatsoever. This poses quite a problem since their husbands may be consumed with lust. If your stitches are fully healed, and for the vast majority of you they will be, the only sensible thing to do is buy some KY jelly or similar, apply liberally and get on with it. Rest assured that nobody has a rip-roaring sex life and a new baby at the same time. It might be worth considering why not.

Most women are simply very tired indeed after six weeks of broken nights – and chronic sleep deprivation is no aphrodisiac. Many do not feel sexually attractive in themselves, especially if they are still overweight and particularly if they are lactating. A common experience of women with new babies is that their breasts leak in an off-putting fashion during sex (especially so if they experience one of those rarities of the postnatal period – an orgasm). There is also always the risk that the baby will start to cry while you are ensconced. Perhaps most insidiously of all, the sexual demands of the husband come across as just that – demands. At a time when the baby is making substantial claims on a mother's time and energy, another person insisting upon physical contact sometimes feels too much for the woman.

For most young families, the early months after the first few postnatal days are quite a strain. At the heart of this is the problem of three people learning to live together as a family where previously there were only two. It is hard enough for two people to learn to live together as a couple (remember all those rows!). Now the task is more complicated. One of the reasons for this is that not only is there a third person in the family but the family roles of the adults have doubled up: each is now not only a wife or husband but a parent, too (as well as often having a career). It is not always clear which role takes priority. The problem over sex is a common flash-point for a row about this competition for role priorities ('You spend all your time worrying about the baby; I need some of you too'). And if, by chance, you find yourselves in a potentially romantic moment and your baby starts to cry, it becomes clear that the mother role trumps the lover role when small babies are concerned.

Learning to live as a three-person, two-generation household is fulfilling but not necessarily easy. It is particularly difficult when you, as the mother/wife (and, yes, the cook, cleaner, shopper, telephone answering service, daughter, daughter-in-law, person-wanted-back-at-the-office, etc.), are beginning to feel increasingly overwhelmed and tired as you find yourself entirely surrounded by baby. It is even tougher if your baby is a prickly, dissatisfied individual rather than one possessing an easy-going, sunny disposition. (See page 204.)

# LOOKING AFTER YOURSELF

There are some things you can do to ease the situation. In essence, many of these mean taking the trouble to look after yourself. If you can do this, you will feel less drained, more resourceful and therefore not so resentful at having to devote some of your time to your husband. This means that he, in turn, will not feel so crabby at having to run around supporting you. If you feel that life is on your side, you can afford to be generous-minded, and this brings back dividends in any relationship.

There is a general risk that, because of the demands of your baby, your own sources of stimulation, which kept you an interesting person in the past, will wither because you can't get to them. You won't want to leave your baby for an evening out at the cinema or theatre, and going out to dinner seems an awe-inspiring organisational challenge. (In any case, will you be able to stay awake until the pudding?) It may, in fact, be easier to have a friend or two over to an unceremonious supper than go out, if only because you can control the timetable.

The odds are that your state of mind is not suited to reading the Booker Prize shortlist in between feeds, but you may be able to read a newspaper. Try to keep your brain ticking over so that you have something to talk about apart from your baby. If there is a way in which you can manage to have something to look forward to each day (a friend coming over, buying yourself something new), you will stave off the comfortable, though suffocating, monotony that is otherwise so easy to sink into.

## Maintaining your social network and your own identity

Women with new babies can become lonely, perhaps for the first time in their lives. They can also, believe it or not, feel slightly bored. At this stage of your life it is really important that you find some soulmates who have babies the same age. You love your baby (in fact, by now you can't imagine life without him) but you are likely to be desperately in need of some fun. Social isolation can creep up on you if you become too obsessed by babycare, and social contacts are an extremely important source of stimulation, which can be lost without you noticing.

With any luck, your antenatal group will provide one or two like-minded mothers who you can have a laugh or moan with. If you haven't already done this, now is the time to see the other people in your class, so make the effort to go to any postnatal classes or reunions. It is also the time to nurture your social network by keeping links with your old friends.

Mates enable you to do things for yourself. If you go shopping together, a friend with a baby can mind them both and utter judgements as you try on various garments. Even better, a friend can look after your baby while you get your hair, legs or nails done. You could go swimming with another mother who also has a baby about the same age, and take it in turns to look after the babies while you each do a couple of lengths. It's really quite important to keep yourself in focus and maintain your own identity as well as caring for your baby.

## Fatigue

You might feel that it's easy to go along with the above, but the fact is tiny babies are tiring. **It is usual for new mothers to hit a trough of exhaustion 10 weeks after the birth.** It may creep up on them unawares because they allow their standards to drift. A night in which they are only woken once for a feed becomes a 'really good night', even if total sleep time is six and a half hours in two stages.

Firstly, you must still try to get some sleep during the day, even if you feel you can do without it. If you are unable to sleep, practise the relaxation techniques you may have been taught at your antenatal classes. Most babies do not sleep through the night until they are about three to four months old – in spite of what other mothers might tell you – and therefore your sleep deprivation will continue to accumulate. If your baby seems to make it impossible for you to sleep during the day, explore the possibility of one of your family or a friend looking after him for a couple of hours once or twice a week.

At the same time, think what other tasks can be delegated: walking up and down with a fretting baby is one. Don't make the mistake of feeling that you will be less than perfect if you don't do everything for your baby yourself. Even breast-feeding needs to be considered in this light. If you are desperately tired after six weeks (especially if you are shortly expected to be back at work) and are satisfactorily breast-feeding, for goodness' sake consider the advantages of combining breast during the day with a bottle at night. This will enable you and your husband to share the joy of night feeds.

At around six weeks it is a good idea in any case to introduce a bottle for one feed a day. It is probably best for this to be expressed breast milk because of the small risk of compromising your milk supply, but if this is impractical or simply too much hassle, you might decide to use formula milk. Unless a bottle is offered regularly you may experience the common problem of your baby losing the skill of teat-sucking between the ages of seven and 11 weeks. You do not want the nightmare of work expecting you back and a baby who is hooked onto the breast and refusing to take a bottle.

If you and your husband are going to share any task which involves getting up at night, the best advice is to have a system of nights 'on duty'. This avoids the business of each partner waking but pretending to be asleep when the baby cries, waiting for the other one to go and deal with the problem, so that in the end two adults have lost the same amount of sleep unnecessarily. It is easier for both of you to agree on who is going to do what beforehand.

Use weekends to catch up on sleep, and for your husband to spend some time with his baby. While you need to keep your social life actively ticking over, avoid late nights out, never go out two evenings running and be wary of long drives to see the baby's grandparents.

## Your weight

Some women are lucky enough to return quickly to more or less the same size and shape after pregnancy as they were before. However, many women put on more weight during pregnancy than they want. At six weeks after having a baby, about half of all new mothers will have a stone to lose in order to regain their pre-pregnancy weight. It can take a long time to come off. Others put on comparatively little during their pregnancy but put it on while they are breast-feeding. Pictures of thin celebs (with masses of money, time and childcare) on the front page of magazines three weeks after the birth of their baby really don't help, and you will be tempted to shed any extra weight as soon as possible. But now is really not the time to try.

It is usually quite difficult to lose weight while you are breast-feeding. You will be hungry because you need a few extra calories to make the milk, and you may have specific cravings, particularly for sweet things. You will also be tired. Dieting as well as dealing with a new baby will just make you miserable and, if you're like most women, you probably won't succeed at this stage in any case. Remind yourself that people who are losing weight feel less cheerful than those who are maintaining a weight. Is now the time to start feeling less happy? Feeling better about being thinner will not, at this stage, outweigh the mood change which is likely to occur if you start losing weight now.

Put the flab problem out of your mind until your baby is six months old. Only if you are still more than about 7 lbs overweight at this time should you put yourself on to a serious diet or book into a weight-loss class.

Try to make yourself feel better about your current size by smartening yourself up. That way you are more likely to collect a few positive remarks about yourself. The alternative – dressing down to the level of a lumpen slob and acting out the way you feel – ought, in theory, to elicit reassurance and expressions of sympathy but actually doesn't work too well. More usually it is just a way of punishing your self-esteem. If you feel that needs deflating, go for it. Otherwise, put on a show at the size you are.

If you can afford it, go and buy some new clothes for yourself (not your baby) that are not too tight. Struggling into trousers with the zip undone and a large pin holding them together at the top is just as depressing as still having to wear maternity clothes when your baby is six weeks old. Be very careful that your body posture does not reflect the fact that you might feel lumpy – make sure you stand tall with your tummy muscles in and your shoulders down and back. It goes without saying that you must find time to wash your hair, have it cut and put on reasonably clean clothes (the ones without regurgitated milk on the shoulder).

Continue to be aware of your body posture, not only because this will make you look better, but because maintaining a good posture is central in avoiding aches and pains. Your posture reflects the way you feel about yourself and by improving your posture you feel better. Check your image in shop windows when you take your baby for a walk. Inspect other pram-pushers critically: have they grasped all this?

## Your pelvic floor – the elevator exercise

You should now have your pelvic floor under something resembling control. Once you can stop the flow of urine during a pee you can start a daily 'elevator' exercise. Contract your pelvic floor muscles in stages. Start by pulling up to the first floor, hold momentarily, then to the second floor, hold and relax. When you have mastered this, add the third floor, so that you go up in three stages. But instead of relaxing completely after reaching the third floor, hold, and then go down in only two stages. The going down bit is rather more difficult so only pause once.

It goes without saying that you will also be continuing your 50 pelvic floor lifts (10 times five plus five) a day and your slow contractions can now be sustained for at least a count of 10.

# YOUR HUSBAND

It is not always easy to keep a focus on your husband. It may seem to you that he is a grown-up and well able to look after himself. Yet you feel guilty when you realise you have been too swamped by babycare to organise an evening meal when he comes in tired after a day's work. You also may find yourself unable to discover any interest whatsoever in his daytime activities when he describes them. This sort of thing tends to become intensified when each party tries to coerce the other into a one-down position, often along the lines of, 'I've had a dreadful day; you should have been able to tell; you would have been able to tell if you'd paid me any attention; it's all your fault I'm upset; now it's up to you to make me feel better', etc. The adult way of managing such conflict is to spot it coming and not get sucked into it.

In very general terms, being open and explicit about how you are feeling is better than playing the game of waiting for the other person to guess, and building up smouldering resentment when they seem to be slow on the uptake. Try to tell your other half straightforwardly how you are feeling (but without playing excessively for sympathy), and ask them to do something specific that will help you (such as walk the baby for a bit).

The whole problem is compounded by the fact that most babies, between the ages of three and 10 weeks, are at their worst in the evening, often just at the time that their fathers return home (see page 143). Some babies will have colic (see pages 146 and 216). This means that parents cannot even sit down together for supper in peace. There is no magic answer to all this and the period from three weeks to three months after birth is likely to be a difficult patch for everyone. It helps if both parents realise that their first duty is to survive, meaning that they grit their teeth and get on with it. It is a strain on individuals and on marriages, but it gets better, it really does.

## YOUR BABY – STARTING SOME GOOD HABITS

At six weeks you can begin to shift the balance of power. Hitherto you have been running very much on your baby's timetable, responsive to his needs at the time they arise. You can now try, gently and gradually, to move these feeding and sleeping requirements into a more predictable pattern – or a loose 'routine'. But because babies are all very different individuals rather than little clones, his routine must reflect his personality and needs as well as yours. You can't force a baby to have a long nap at precisely 11 o'clock in the morning if his natural rhythm is to have a long nap in the early afternoon. Likewise, forcing a baby with reflux into a strict feeding routine would be cruel. Ideally you should strive towards taking charge, but be 'baby-led' (rather than book-led) as far as the details are concerned.

The point of predictable feeding and sleeping times is to help you manage your life, keep yourself in focus, have fun with your baby and help him to thrive. **Be very careful not to become routine-obsessed** so that this dominates your life and has the reverse effect. You don't want either your baby's demands or his 'routine' to take complete control over you.

## FEEDING

As far as feeding goes, most bottle-fed babies will by now be on a predictable three and a half- or four-hour pattern. Many breast-fed babies will also have organised themselves into a similar pattern, having six, or later on, five feeds during a 24-hour period. Other breast-fed babies will be hopelessly unpredictable or, worse still, continue to want feeding every two and a half hours. If their weight gain is good, these latter babies will be taking the right amount of milk over 24 hours (so you are producing the required quantity) but in smaller, more frequent amounts.

Provided that your baby's weight gain is satisfactory (around 15 oz or 450 g a fortnight), now is the time to start the business of establishing a feeding pattern. Just watch out for the possibility that your baby is going through a minor greedy patch (as a result of a growth spurt) when he demands (and needs) more milk. This is something which tends to happen for a few days at about five to six weeks and again at nine to 10 weeks. You will know when it happens because your breasts will be less full than usual and your baby will not settle after a feed. Avoid introducing a routine at this particular point – feed your baby more frequently and your breasts will get the message that they need to produce more milk. This will take two to three days.

Otherwise, over the next week or so, aim to lengthen gradually the time between his feeds. Incidentally, in order for him to take the five feeds he needs during the daytime, he has to have his first feed not much later than 7am, waking him if necessary. The sixth, and for some, the seventh feed will be during the night, between 7pm and 7am. Find two days that are reasonably clear of commitments. Perhaps start by setting a minimum of three hours between feeds during the daytime (between 7am and 7pm), forgetting about the evenings and nights for the time being.

If your baby starts to agitate two and a half hours after the beginning of the last breast-feed, don't opt for the easy solution of putting him to the breast but work away with distraction techniques – jiggling him, taking him for a walk or car ride, or even giving him a bath. Keep stringing him out to a minimum of three hours between the starts of successive daytime feeds.

Once he is comfortably established on a three-hour minimum interval during the day for at least three days continuously, you can move to setting the minimum at three and a quarter hours between feeds. Once he has settled on that for three days, move to three and a half hours between feeds. You can afford to be flexible about the timing of early evening feeds. If he has colic in the evenings, wait until this subsides at about 12 weeks before trying to fiddle with evening feed timings.

# SLEEPING

## Daytime sleeps

If you make a point of ensuring that your baby is put down lying flat for his daytime sleeps (as opposed to sitting slumped in the car seat), you have a better chance of him avoiding the catnap syndrome of short, unsustained spells of sleep. This is the situation in which he naps for brief periods during the day, dozing off in the car seat for five minutes, and is then woken as you sweep him indoors and whisk his hat off, putting him in a bouncing chair while you unload the washing machine. He dozes again, subsequently being jolted awake by you scooping him up to take him upstairs for his afternoon nap (while you have yours), whereupon he doesn't (and neither do you). He never gets the chance to get into a good habit of sustained sleep.

**In our experience the vast majority of first-born babies are over-stimulated and over-tired. It does sound odd,**

but, generally speaking, a baby who sleeps well during the day will sleep better at night. It is wrong (but sometimes suggested) to try to keep a baby awake all day in the belief he will sleep longer at night: he won't. And an over-tired baby will not be able to take a good feed because the sucking will make him fall asleep.

Help your baby to learn how to settle himself to sleep at least twice during the day. Babies normally wake at night, even when they are not hungry. They then need to know how to get back to sleep on their own, and this is a skill they have to learn. Otherwise they are dependent on you to help them fall asleep. A baby will find it easier to settle himself back to sleep at night if he has learnt how to fall asleep on his own during the day. This means putting him down for a good horizontal sleep at least twice during the day. He doesn't have to be in his or your bedroom, and he doesn't need complete darkness or total silence.

If he is difficult to settle, swaddle him tightly, give him a dummy if he likes it, and lie him in his pram or bouncy cradle in a flat position. Stand or sit out of his line of sight, because your face is very exciting for him and in no way sleep-inducing (remember that your face is the most stimulating toy he has at the moment). For a similar reason don't stroke his face when trying to settle him. Rhythmically rock or jiggle the pram or chair. You will probably have to rock or jiggle for much longer than you would like.

If you always pace up and down the room with him in your arms to settle him, he will come to think that he is only able to fall asleep when you're holding him, so when he wakes in the night your arms won't be there; they will be trying to get some sleep with the rest of you! Help him to learn how to settle himself. You can let him cry a bit at such times, so long as he doesn't get too fraught. Just keep gently and gradually encouraging him to do what you want him to do.

Once again, don't be too impatient with colicky babies. Because they inevitably spend every evening being paced until they settle, they have less opportunity to learn how to fall asleep alone. There's nothing you should do about this beyond trying to create that opportunity during the day when settling them for a nap. Don't try to give up pacing in the evenings. The colic will have disappeared by 14 weeks and you can sort things out once it has done so.

Avoid out-and-out confrontations because these don't help him learn new skills – at this age he is far too young to be 'taught' that he has to go to sleep in certain situations – such as when it is past 8pm. You might think it necessary or helpful to demonstrate to him that you are in charge, but it won't actually make any difference to him at this age, though it may well result in you losing confidence. He won't learn that he is less powerful than you because he can't yet think like that.

## Helping your baby to sleep through the night(!)

Small babies sleep for more hours in the day than adults but they have not yet learned the cues which induce sleep at night rather than in the day. For the first few weeks after birth their sleep/wake cycle is independent of night and day, and they only slowly learn a pattern of one major sleep session at night and two or three shorter ones during the day. If you allow your baby a protracted sleep of six hours during the day you may find that he is shifting his major sleep session into daylight hours with interesting periods of alert sociability in the small hours of the morning.

For such reasons it is wise to wake him after three hours of continuous sleep in any daytime nap – and for the same reason not to wake him after 7pm during the night. Nearly all mothers find that things work better if they allow the baby to wake spontaneously for night feeds.

Most babies don't start to sleep through the night (a decent stretch of 10 to 12 hours) until around three months. With any luck, between the age of seven and 10 weeks, he will manage to sleep for at least a six-hour stretch, provided he is having enough milk during the day. Very roughly speaking, at this stage, babies can sleep at night the same amount of hours as their age in weeks. Unless, that is, they are underweight, were premature or born very small, or have reflux. The problem might be that you find it is the 'wrong' stretch (between 8pm and 3am, for example) and wonder whether to wake him for a 10pm feed before you go to bed. In the long run, most mothers discover it is best not to.

Although the temptation to wake him up before you crash out is hard to resist, what seems to happen is that, having been woken, he is sleepy(!) and therefore does not take as much milk as he would have had he woken on his own. So he still wakes for a feed later during the night because he is hungry. Another problem is that if he is difficult to settle after a 10pm feed you may be up till midnight (and he still wakes at 3am).

During the period of 10 weeks onwards his sleeping time will lengthen as a matter of course. If you keep waking him up in the night you may well mess this up because you won't be giving him the opportunity to go for a longer period between his night-time feeds. If you allow him to wake spontaneously, what you will probably find is that he naturally lengthens the interval between feeds all on his own.

You will probably have noticed that there is a helpful interplay between the development of longer sleep–wake cycles and longer feed–hunger cycles. Waking him for a night feed interferes with this and will make it more difficult for him to adjust to longer periods between night feeds, which is the necessary preparation before dropping a night feed altogether. As babies get bigger they can take more milk at a feed. But they don't suddenly sleep for eight hours; they gradually lengthen the time they are content to go without food. Therefore, before he gives up demanding a night feed, you are likely to have a few unsatisfactory weeks when he wakes at a worse time than usual – say at 5am rather than at 3am. Although this is pretty exhausting for you, remember that it will not be forever and is actually a step in the right direction.

If you are fortunate enough to have a baby who sleeps for a 12-hour stretch at night, remember that it will be impossible to fit in five feeds at four-hour intervals during the day. You may find you have to reduce the four-hour interval between feeds, rather than dropping to four feeds, as most babies are happier on five feeds during a 24-hour period at this stage.

## DEVELOPMENTAL CHECKS

It used to be the case that babies were taken to a children's doctor in a community clinic for developmental checks at frequent intervals. In some areas this is still done by a paediatrician at a child health clinic but elsewhere it will be your GP. The older, rather rigid system of regular developmental checks has been replaced by a more flexible approach, but most doctors will want to check your baby's development at eight weeks when they will offer immunisation at the same time (see below).

# IMMUNISATION

At eight weeks your baby is due for his first two immunisation injections:

- DTaP/IPV/Hib (one injection, usually given into his thigh):
  - DTaP against diphtheria, tetanus and pertussis (whooping cough)
  - IPV against polio
  - Hib against the haemophilus bacterium, which is one of the causes of meningitis, pneumonia and ear infections.
- PCV against the pneumococcus bacterium (which can cause meningitis and pneumonia) in another injection at the same visit.

This is the first immunisation visit. There will be others that are necessary, the next ones being at 12 and 16 weeks.

Immunisation is a wonderful thing. The diseases that it protects against can kill babies. They used to and they still do. You may have heard horror stories about the side-effects of the older immunisation agents and be apprehensive accordingly. The problem is that you may not have heard the stories about the children who get the infections which could have been prevented by immunisation. We have all become used to a world in which most babies survive and thrive. Yet part of the reason for this is immunisation, which has rendered most of the childhood population immune, so that the diseases in question have become rare. Most people in the Western world will not have seen the awful tragedy of a baby dying of diphtheria or meningitis, and paralysis caused by polio is a thing of the past. Yet it is not so long ago that most babies who died had infections that can now be prevented. Indeed, preventative immunisation is the only treatment for diseases caused by viruses like polio since antibiotics do not work on viruses.

Some people say that they feel immunisation is not 'natural' and that their baby would be better off without it. Yet natural things are not necessarily safe, whether they be laburnum seeds or meningitis bacteria.

You may also not be aware of the recent advances made in vaccine preparation. Modern baby vaccines are very, very much less likely to cause side-effects than those of 10 years or so ago, and the ones routinely used no longer contain mercury. The risks from not having your baby immunised are far greater than any minuscule risk from the immunisation. Although many mothers expect some side-effects from an immunisation, these are unusual beyond some grizzling extending into the next day. In fact, this usually means the vaccine has produced an inflammatory reaction indicating it has effectively stimulated immunity (but don't panic if there are no side-effects). The routine immunisations given to your baby will not overwhelm his immune system, nor will they cause fits, brain damage, autism or asthma. There are nowadays virtually no medical contra-indications to routine immunisation.

# CHAPTER 14:
## Three months onwards

This section concentrates more on you as the parents (and especially you as the mother) than on your baby. He will change enormously now and quickly learn an amazing number of skills – including putting everything into his mouth. All of this you will probably monitor with the help of a baby book, and you will check his progress against your friends' babies in spite of your secret conviction that he is streets ahead of every other baby.

At about 14 weeks, you are likely to start feeling less tired and rather more in control of things. You have, in fact, survived the worst of the sleep deprivation and your quality of life should be improving. By now you may have a baby who settles at about seven o'clock in the evening and thus you will have a little time for yourself. But in spite of this, you may find it surprisingly difficult to use the time for creative leisure opportunities. A number of women may secretly be feeling seriously drained and flat. Looking after a baby is an awful lot of work and even though your baby will be the best thing that has ever happened to you, getting through the days can seem a bit of a slog. Thinking back to how things were before you were pregnant may induce a sensation of unreality – was it really once possible that you did a full day's work, had a swim and then went out for dinner? You have become a skilled mother but you will not yet have picked up the threads of your earlier life.

Your husband is back at his work and has probably re-engaged in it just as much as before the birth. He has accommodated to his baby and accepted his new status as a father. For him the baby is (a wonderful) part of the home set-up, and you might be secretly irritated that for him it has all been rather easy and that he can get away from it all. If his work means he has to spend nights away from home, you might also be alarmed to discover that you now feel uneasy in the house at night on your own.

To you he probably seems much less engrossed by your baby and less involved in babycare than you are. He may let slip that he is a bit fed up at your preoccupation with the baby and would appreciate your rediscovery of sexual recreation. But for you sex is almost certainly not at the top of your list of priorities and quite possibly not on it at all. He wants to know why you have changed, whether and when you are going to be your old self again, and he might even accuse you of being boring. Indeed, at times you may feel a little jaded or even bored yourself.

Yet there are some extraordinary moments of pride, love and satisfaction. At some stage in the next few weeks you will realise that you have accomplished the tasks involved in the first part of becoming a parent. You aren't ever going to be your old self again; you will be your old self transformed.

# PELVIC FLOOR

Continue your exercises (10 times five plus five, daily) until you have a perfect pelvic floor. It takes around six months of regular exercising following a normal delivery and three months following a Caesarean section for your muscles to return to their pre-pregnancy strength.

Try to do your exercises while:
- feeding
- standing in a checkout queue
- waiting for websites to download
- stuck at red traffic lights
- talking to someone very boring
- waiting on the phone ('Your call is very important to us...').

You will know you have a perfect (or pretty good) pelvic floor when you can:
- maintain a contraction for a count of 30 seconds
- take your pelvic floor up five floors and down four floors (see page 128)
- stop the flow of urine midstream – however full your bladder
- with a full bladder, jump several times with your legs apart while coughing, and remain dry
- make your husband gasp.

Wise women who can do all this will continue to do 10 lifts a day for the rest of their lives as a 'well woman' exercise to keep the muscles in good working order. It doesn't take a genius to realise that these muscles play a major role in your sex life. It might also be worth taking the view that toned pelvic floor muscles are the best insurance against future problems – no woman in her sixties, let alone fifties, expects to wear a pad because she leaks wee when she coughs or laughs.

If you are experiencing any trouble such as leaking urine, or pain when you have sex, consult your GP. It's probable that the above exercises will sort things out by the time your baby is six months old, but if not, you will almost certainly need to be referred to a gynaecologist. You are absolutely not expected to put up with any 'problems below' just because you have had a baby.


## THINKING ABOUT RETURNING TO WORK

Some people have no choice as to whether or not to go back to work. Others have the luxury of a choice but are not sure of the right thing to do. One of the most difficult decisions that a new mother has to make is whether she is the type of woman who wants to be at home with her baby while he is growing up, or whether she is happier working.

There are no rights and wrongs in all this, and it is impossible to know which group you fall into until you have had your baby. Even then, you won't necessarily know what is right for you until you have actually tried returning to work. For some women, full-time mother-hood is just not for them. The guiding principle is that a happy mother is usually a good mother, and there are those who are not happy unless working, just as there are women who are only happy if they spend all their time with their baby.

If the mother has a satisfying job which boosts her self-esteem, then her child will benefit indirectly. Children's self-esteem derives principally from their parents' self-esteem, and an adequate sense of self-worth is an important element in preventing emotional complications during development.

Of course, for a number of women, bringing up a baby is a rewarding task in its own right and they will derive more than enough pride in themselves from just that. But there are others who need the stimulation (or the money) gained from paid work as well as the social status that, unfortunately, goes with it.

# GETTING ORGANISED

Much of the early part of this book is about planning, managing and getting organised, and you may have skipped some of it if you found it all a turn-off. But if you are going back to work at this stage, getting organised is essential. You simply have to make arrangements ahead of time instead of being reactive to circumstances. Diaries and lists are crucial for your survival. If it's too difficult, think about whether you really should be going back to work now. You're in control and perhaps you can put things off without losing your place on the career ladder, or you might even give in your notice and change direction. There is no absolute right thing to do that suits everybody, and it may be better to fix a later date in your mind for going back. The important thing is not to drift or panic, and make sure you discuss all options with your husband. We have given the topic of returning to work quite a lot of space (see also page 191) because it is so challenging, but that doesn't mean that everyone has to do it. You might make an active decision not to do so (or to do so at a later date).

## CONTINUING TO MAINTAIN YOUR RELATIONSHIP WITH YOUR HUSBAND

There is a sizeable chance that your husband is experiencing your divided attention. Babies are experts in attracting attention and accordingly will muscle in on any act whenever they have the chance. They are often quite greedy about it, too. Your baby is not likely to say, in so many words, 'Go on, talk to him, don't mind me. I'll amuse myself quietly for an hour or so.' Yet somehow you have to deal with a husband who is likely to be feeling excluded from your attention and affections, who can feel irritated by this and may be almost as tired as you are from getting up at night. Somehow you need to manage to give your husband your *un*divided attention from time to time in order for your relationship to flourish rather than deteriorate. And he needs to manage to give you some undivided attention, too. Are you making it possible for him to do this? In order for it to happen, you will both have to get away from your baby to allow yourselves to go out together for a walk, a meal, or any other activity involving no more than the two of you.

You also need to maintain your own identity. You continue to need some time and space for yourself to keep up your old interests, to look after your appearance and to remind yourself that you are someone in your own right as well as being a mother. If you can do this, you will feel (and be) attractive and interesting to everyone else – including your husband.

### Weekends

To help you to do some of the above, your husband may be able to take the baby off your hands for extended intervals at weekends. He might relish the pride that goes with sole responsibility for his baby during that time. But this isn't always the case. People are different and some fathers like being part of a family group, while others would rather be on their own with their babies (or in their office). Nevertheless, if you can take turns with babycare duties, you should each be able to get some extra sleep, if you need it. If he takes the baby out, you can crash out, and later, you can do the same for him. On the other hand you may simply enjoy being on your own for a while, knowing that your baby is in safe hands. It is different from having him tag along with you and the baby all the time, which can easily make some fathers feel like an accessory.

Be cautious of going away to stay with friends or family at weekends – it is often not the rest you anticipated. If you are not in your own home, it is much harder for each of you to peel off in turn from the socialising. Do not despair about any residual fatigue. Your energy levels will eventually return to normal (until you get pregnant again).

If you have weaned your baby from the breast, then there is an opportunity for both you and your husband to get completely away. You will certainly not scar your baby for life if you both bunk off for a night or two, leaving him with his grandparents. It may be just as much fun to leave him with them at their house in order to have a weekend on your own at home. Some people also discover that leaving their baby with their parents for a couple of nights may cure an otherwise stubborn bad sleep habit! Going off for a week's skiing or shopping in New York is probably less of a good idea, though – too long and too far away. If there is a person who suffers it is going to be you, racked with guilt and separation anxiety. Babies are well able to tolerate brief separations from their parents in the first five months of their lives, though from about six months they start to develop a particular sort of emotional attachment to you, which means that they will become anxious and distressed if you leave them. With this in mind it is better to go for several two-day breaks in the first year rather than a protracted holiday.

## MAINTAINING YOUR NETWORKS

Although you need to get out of the house from time to time, the advice not to go out socialising two nights running is so important we are repeating it. It's often very difficult to decline an invitation, especially if your self-assertion skills are not yet up to capacity, but don't get bullied into accepting. Babies always seem to sense that you have had a late night by choosing to have a very early morning. It's extraordinary how quickly even friends with children of their own can forget how necessary it is for you to make sleep a priority in these first few months.

If you are not working, make a special effort to keep up with girlfriends – in particular, those who stimulate you. (This is advice for mothers, not fathers!)

If you are having people for supper, you don't need to prepare a gourmet meal. Have the confidence to keep everything straightforward and expend only minimal effort on preparation. Don't apologise for simple food, serve good wine and try to keep your baby out of the way for most of the time.

# YOUR BABY

## Medical checks

When your baby is 12 weeks old and again at 16 weeks, his second and third immunisations are due.

## Feeding

You may notice that the rate of his weight gain slows down at about this time but this is not likely to be a cause for alarm if your baby is feeding satisfactorily and is well in other respects. Look at your baby rather than the book.

Most bottle-fed babies will be taking four bottles during the day at this stage. A few breast-fed babies will also manage to thrive on four breast-feeds, but most will need five. The timing of feeds will need to be condensed during the day with an early start (i.e. between the hours of 7am and 7–8pm), otherwise you are going to be feeding him in the night (see page 166). What you are aiming to do is encourage your baby to move towards taking all his calories during waking hours (like children and adults) rather than at regular intervals across an entire 24-hour period. If he is on four feeds, the timing is relatively easy – say 7am, 11am, 2.30pm and 6.15pm. If he needs five feeds rather than four, the interval between the feeds will need to be roughly three to three and a half hours rather than four hours, or you will not have enough daytime hours to fit them all in. You may end up with a feeding pattern along these lines: 7am, 10am, 1.30pm, 4.30pm and 7.30pm.

## WEANING ONTO FORMULA MILK

Some mothers (especially those who know they have to go back to work) will want to wean their babies onto formula milk at around three months. The best way to start is by replacing a midday or mid-morning breast-feed with a formula feed. Then after three days (to allow your breasts to get the message that they are no longer required to produce milk for this feed) replace another feed (preferably not the one directly before or after the one you have just dropped) with another formula feed, and so on . . .

## INTRODUCING SOLID FOOD

Your baby is ready to start some solid food when he needs more calories than he can get from milk alone. He will let you know when this happens by demanding extra feeds during the day, and/or he may start waking earlier in the morning, hungry and unable to hang on until his usual breakfast feed-time.

Babies need to start taking solid food somewhere between four and six months. Advice on precise timing seems to vary with fashion on a 20-year cycle. Breast or formula milk will give your baby all the nutrition he needs for up to six months; indeed, the World Health Organization currently recommends delaying the introduction of solid food until then. Some of the baby police take this as rigid doctrine and do not consider the individual baby. In practice, most mothers consider their babies are ready to start some solid food at around four to five months. There are some very hungry babies who need solid food supplementation even earlier – perhaps at 14 weeks.

As well as giving your baby extra calories, another reason for starting solid food is to encourage the natural progression from sucking to chewing – it is not just to 'fill him up' so he sleeps longer during the night. **At this stage, solid food is always offered in addition to his usual amount of milk** (not instead of it) and given from a spoon, never from a bottle. Babies take some time to master this new technique and can bite the spoon by mistake, so you need to use a special plastic or wooden type without sharp edges. The spoon and bowl do not need sterilising.

Most mothers start with baby rice (mixed with breast or formula milk or water) and baby jars of puréed fruit. Introduce solid food slowly, a few spoonfuls halfway through a milk feed. If he doesn't like it or can't manage a spoon, leave it for a week. Respect the inevitable conservatism of a baby and his particular taste preferences; it is best not to introduce a new food more often than once every three days – otherwise if there is something that doesn't agree with him, you won't know what it is.

Initially, it is better to start with bought food rather than something you have lovingly prepared yourself and puréed – that comes later. There are two reasons for this. Firstly, baby-food manufacturers are good at knowing what babies like, which is important if the procedure is to be a pleasurable experience for you both. They have to be careful that their food has all the appropriate vitamins in it, too, so don't worry on that score. In any case, at the moment your baby is just learning a new skill, rather than being dependent on solids for his nutrition. Secondly, for the first week or so, he will be taking such small quantities that you will find yourself throwing away quite a bit. No one likes throwing away food that they have spent time (and love) preparing, so you may be tempted to 'encourage' your baby to take more than he wants and subsequently put him off the whole business.

Ordinarily speaking, you don't have to think about adding vitamins, iron or fluoride supplements to a baby's diet before he is six months old.

# DUMMIES

Earlier in this book (see page 91) we advocated a dummy as a useful way of helping your baby to soothe himself so that you did not have to do this for him, particularly when settling him to sleep. From about four months on, a baby can successfully put and keep his fingers or thumb in his mouth so that he no longer needs a dummy to suck for self-soothing. Most babies will therefore discard their dummies of their own accord between three and five months. The occasional baby will show no signs of this and you may feel it's time to wean him off. You don't have to, but might want to if you find yourself plugging in a lost dummy several times a night. You could try not giving it to him during the day, and leaving him to use or develop other ways of settling himself. Some babies are not going to accept this move and, if you feel strongly about seeing it through (and when you feel tough enough to cope), you may have to brace yourself for a few days of protest by imposing cold turkey and throwing the dummy away.

# SLEEPING

It has been said (by a mother of four) that you love your babies in direct proportion to the amount of sleep they allow you to have. You might empathise with this.

You may be unlucky and have a well-grown and healthy baby who just doesn't sleep well, but with a bit of luck, a 14-week-old baby will be going to bed at around 7pm and going through the night without demanding a night feed. Provided he is over 13 lb (6 kg) in weight, he is probably able to, although he may be waking earlier than you would like. If he is still waking in the small hours, you will probably be very keen to change this pattern by now.

There are five common reasons for him waking (and crying) in the night:

- unwell
- too cold
- hungry
- teething
- no problem, but he doesn't settle himself back to sleep.

An unwell baby obviously needs attention, cuddles and reassurance during the night until he gets better. For a baby who regularly kicks off his blankets, it might be worth trying a baby sleeping bag.

## Is he hungry?

Is his weight gain OK? If he knocks back 6 oz (175 ml) of milk when he wakes in the night, he is clearly hungry and needs the calories in the milk. Somehow, you need to give him more milk during the daytime. If he only takes 2 oz (60 ml), he is clearly not very hungry, and you could try to settle him with a bottle containing warm water (rather than milk) because that will not interfere with his calorie intake the next day.

## Is he teething?

Babies start to teethe as early as 14 weeks and sometimes even earlier. Although a few babies show no outward signs of teething and their first tooth simply appears (at any time after four months), many are bothered by sore gums over the growing tooth before this. The signs of a baby who is teething are:

- dribbling
- constantly chewing his hands
- sometimes slightly flushed cheeks
- waking in the night.

**Teething is not responsible for a baby having a temperature.** Sometimes it is helpful to give your baby Calpol (or similar) before he goes down for the night, and repeat the dose if he wakes in the night. Grit your own teeth and remind yourself that teething does not last forever. Eventually the tooth will come through (unfortunately to be followed in quick succession by another but with luck there will be a break in between).

## He can't settle himself back to sleep once he has woken

As it happens, all babies wake during the night, but only some cry. If your baby has not yet learned how to settle back to sleep on his own and cries for his mother to make a nipple or teat available for him to soothe himself (or find the lost dummy), the problem is not, therefore, so much that he wakes, rather that he cannot get himself back off to sleep. When you have excluded the other possible reasons (see above) for waking, this is likely to be the problem. The best remedy might be to concentrate on helping your baby learn the skill of settling himself when he has his day-time sleeps. Meanwhile, you have no option but to take alternate nights on duty with your husband, and do what you can to settle him by patting, stroking, rocking or walking him round the room. At this age babies are too young to be left to cry it out for longer than about 20 minutes. (Ignore recommendations about 'controlled crying' at this age – he is too young.) Your first duty is to survive, not to try to change your baby's night-time habits in a fruitless showdown of who breaks first. Things will improve with time.

In general terms, the problem begins to shift from crying at night to difficulty settling him at bedtime. The first thing to do is fix a bedtime at a point in the evening when you are likely to succeed. Make a decision as to when night starts. A good guide is when your baby seems to be sleepy (and you can often miss this magic moment) balanced with what is convenient for you – 7pm suits most families. It isn't usually the case that the later you keep him up the easier it will be to settle him and the later he will sleep in the morning. In practice this yields unpredictable results. Try to stop him falling asleep in the late afternoon and watch out for the common problem of a father returning from work and hyping his baby up by boisterous play.

If you can, always try to settle him in the same room and make it darker than it is during the day (not usually too difficult). That way you can set the environmental cues for him to recognise both that he is expected to go to sleep and whether it is appropriate for him to go back to sleep should he wake. Because babies can't tell the time, it might be worth establishing other evening rituals which act as cues that bedtime is approaching, such as a bath, followed by putting him into a nightie (a more specific cue than putting him into anything which he might wear during the day), and singing a special lullaby. Such routines act as a reassurance to the baby because he knows what sequence to expect and they thus also act as a communication as to what he is expected to do next.

You might want to include a feed in the evening routine, but don't let it end up with him falling asleep at the breast because he needs to develop the skill of falling asleep alone. In the middle of the night the owner of the breast will be getting her own sleep (probably in a different bed) and it will not be there for him to turn to.

# CHAPTER 15:

## Returning to work

### WHEN TO RETURN

You may have no choice of course. But if you do have the luxury of a choice, it's worth bearing in mind that most babies don't sleep through the night until they are at least 14 weeks old. On the other hand, generally speaking, most mothers find it is better to go back to work before their baby is six months old. There are two reasons for this. Firstly, if you let too many months roll by, you become immersed in babycare and lose your confidence for work-related things. Secondly, at about six months of age, babies begin to cling to their mothers and cry bitterly at separation from them. This is normal separation anxiety and signifies their development of a selective emotional attachment to you. It will happen whether or not you return to work, and will apply to separations around the home (such as your going to the loo). But if you start leaving the house to go to work at the same time as your baby is beginning to show separation anxiety, you will find the wrench almost unbearable. All your guilt buttons will be pressed simultaneously.

# FULL-TIME OR PART-TIME?

Once again, you may have no choice, but it is altogether less stressful if you can return on a part-time or flexi-time basis. Bear in mind that nearly all mothers find working three or four full days and then having a complete day off much easier to manage than five short days. This is because when you leave work at the end of each short day you are actually coming home to more work. The impact of this transition between two work situations is greater than the burden of staying at work for a longer day.

There are going to be days when you have to take time off because your baby is ill or you need to take him to the doctor. Be prepared for your employer to become a little grumpy if you have to take time off for a sick baby – after all, they interviewed you for the job and estimated your fitness for it, not your baby's. You may feel it wise to offer to put in a few extra hours at some stage to compensate for all this.

# WORRIES AND GUILT

The real problem of returning to work lies beyond the practical arrangements. When you are preparing to go back to work you are likely to feel you are being a bad mother. You may panic that you have made the wrong decision, even if it has effectively been made for you. You will probably also be worried as to how you are going to cope on mornings when you have had very little sleep. But most of us can afford to have the odd morning at work when we function a bit below par, and the strange thing is that usually no one notices – we set higher standards for ourselves than are set for us by others. It is a worry that is fuelled by wavering self-confidence – a common enough curse of new motherhood.

You will undoubtedly feel guilty at leaving your baby (especially if you have had to wean him earlier than you would have wanted because of your work) and anxious for his welfare. At any point, you may think: something dreadful will happen to pay me back for abandoning my baby. Yet you will probably not voice such concerns openly because you know in your heart of hearts that they are irrational, so you keep them to yourself. Awkwardly, this makes them persist and keeps you in a state of vulnerability, because you don't take a reality check by discussing them with someone you trust. You remain unsure as to whether you are doing the right thing.

For such reasons you need to be able to count on the unequivocal support of your husband and your parents. A risk is incidental criticism from girlfriends who take an unrealistic view of how much time you should spend with your baby, pontificating accordingly. Your sensitive hearing will pick up even the mildest adverse comment from others. It is important for you to make contacts with other working mothers who will support you, and who will also give you some practical tips.

# PRACTICAL ARRANGEMENTS

## Weaning from the breast

The vast majority of mothers who return to work will need their baby to be feeding only from a bottle during the day. If you are breast-feeding, start the transfer by giving him one bottle-feed a day a full four weeks ahead of your planned return so that you have accomplished the transition to total daytime bottle-feeding at least 10 days before you start back at work.

Daytime bottle-feeding will programme your breasts not to produce milk during the day – the last thing you need in the office, cockpit or classroom. It also gives you time to make sure you feel happy that your baby is taking the bottle cheerfully and not pining for the breast. Even if you are normally level-headed and logical, be prepared to feel a little sad and guilty when you start to wean from breast to bottle, no matter how old your baby is. You can, of course, still continue to breast-feed your baby in the evening and morning.

For many women, having to curtail breast-feeding earlier than they would have liked to is one of the most distressing aspects of returning to work. Although breast milk has a few small nutritional advantages over modern formula milk, this is insignificant by five months. It really isn't necessary to keep disappearing into lavatories to express your own milk into a bottle. If a return to work means that you have to move on to bottle-feeding with formula milk, it will neither impair your relationship with your baby nor prejudice his A-level grades.

## Support from your husband and parents

What you really need now is a wife. It may be a little tricky to sell this idea to your husband. Perhaps he'll read this page. What he is going to have to do is pay more than lip service to your return to work. He will have to listen to your agonising about your decision (see above). And then there is the whole raft of drudgeries to do with running the house, not all of them fascinating, which he will have to give a hand with. You need him to do this without complaining (just like a wife?!). Perhaps some agreed allocation of tasks between you would help clarify matters.

If you are lucky enough to have an available mother yourself this will be wonderful, especially if you have to work evenings or nights.

# CHILDCARE

This is usually your biggest headache and very time-consuming to arrange. But basically what you need is someone who is used to babies, sensible, kind and competent, no more than that. You don't need the services of a consultant paediatrician to look after a baby – even your baby. Nevertheless, plan to spend as much as you can afford on a nanny, childminder or nursery. **Never economise on childcare.** You cannot do your work properly if you are worried about the quality of care your baby is receiving in your absence.

If you can, arrange five-days-a-week care if you are working for as many as four days. You will probably have to do this in any case. It enables you to leave him for a few hours on your 'day off' if you need to.

Childcare is expensive and the cost often needs to be shared between both parents; there is no logical need for it to be borne solely by the mother, though it often is by default. Have low expectations of how much money you will have in your pockets at the end of the month.

Should you be freelance and working at home, don't fall into the trap of thinking you can work and look after the baby at the same time; you won't be able to concentrate and you won't do either job well. You will still need some help with babycare if you are going to be any good at your job. It doesn't mean that you are a better person if you can just about stagger through being both an exhausted, distracted mother and an exhausted, distracted money-earner at the same time.

In fact, there is a general principle here: compartmentalise things and try to create some boundaries around your responsibilities and activities. You *can* do several things at once, but you may find this means that those several things are not done very well. You need to provide your baby with undivided attention from time to time; you need to have time with your husband separately without your baby being there, too; and you need time on your own, so that you can be all the things that you are apart from a mother. If you are at work, then you need to concentrate on work.

If you can afford a nanny, all well and good, but many women will use a childminder or (from six weeks old) a nursery during the working week. There will almost certainly be a local grapevine to be tapped when you are looking for one. Otherwise, all childminders must register with Ofsted and there is a list you can have a look at on the childcarelink website (www.childcare link.gov.uk). If you are fortunate enough to have your baby's grandparents living nearby who offer to look after your baby, do use them. By definition they have brought up at least one infant, are safe, love their grandchild and will play a continuing part in your baby's life.

It very much depends what or who is available in your area, and if you know other working mothers who can advise you. This is another reason why a network of local mates is so important. But decisions about childcare revolve around a number of considerations. One of these is where you want your baby to be while you are working. If he has a nanny, he will be in his own home. If he goes to a childminder, he will be in her house. And if you leave him at a childminder or nursery, he will travel to and from there with you. No one of these alternatives is automatically superior – it depends on what you can afford and what feels best for you; each option has advantages and disadvantages.

## Nannies

This is the most expensive option. Nannies usually live in with you, although it is possible to engage one on a daily basis. A live-in nanny will become part of your family, which can cause the occasional problem in its own right. But if you have room in your flat/house, this has many advantages, because you will see how your nanny and your baby really get on with each other. It also means that you don't have to clock-watch at the end of the working day and you have the advantage of an occasional babysitter in the evenings and some respite on Saturday mornings.

Most mothers find it best to wait until their baby has arrived before they start interviewing. Although (even more) expensive, it is better to go through an agency which will have screened all the candidates. When you think you have found the right person, arrange for her to start as early as you can afford (at least three weeks) before you are due back at work. This gives you time to start leaving your baby for a few hours at a time before leaving him for a whole day (you may need this time in any case to buy some temporary work clothes, because your pre-pregnancy gear still doesn't fit). If you have any misgivings, it also gives you just about enough time to replace her.

## A nursery

As your baby grows older, spending time in the day with other children can be a bonus for his play and social development. There now are a number of very good, amply staffed nurseries that cater for the offspring of working parents, and they open early in the morning. Obviously, you will need to check out what is available in your area, visit them and, if you are happy, book your baby in well in advance.

Once again, think ahead. If you are going to entrust your baby to a nursery, start leaving him for a half-day well before you are due to be back at work, so if you have any misgivings you can find another one.

It might be worth remembering that a caring environment for a group of babies and children is also a caring environment for a number of bacteria and viruses, who will appreciate your provision of a host for their own breeding activities. Yet the coughs and colds that he catches early can build immunity for when he starts school.

## A childminder

This is someone who is registered to look after a small number of babies and children in her own home. The majority of childminders are experienced but unqualified, beyond a basic course including first-aid. They and their homes will have been inspected and they will display a registration certificate on their wall. Again, you need to know via the grapevine who is good (and available) in your area.

# SOME OTHER CONSIDERATIONS

To say the mornings will be busy is an understatement. You will learn to prepare everything the night before and, unless you have a nanny, never run the dishwasher overnight so it needs to be unpacked in the morning.

Keep in mind, though, that nothing is forever. If, when you are back at work, you find it feels wrong, you can always change your mind. You will not be in a position to make a rational decision about working or staying at home until you have tried both. Good luck with whatever you do. Make a date in your diary for six months' time to re-appraise the situation by talking it over with your husband.

# PART FIVE:

## Some Other Things

# CHAPTER 16:

## Your baby's personality

Everyone who has had more than one baby knows that each baby is different. Not just in appearance but in their whole general temperament. Some have a sunny disposition; others are more irritable. Some are placid; others excitable. This inevitably affects how you react to them and also how you feel about yourself. The sort of emotional and behavioural style your baby has is pivotal for your morale as a new parent.

The crucial thing to grasp is that babies are different right from the word go – anyone who has worked with a number of newborn babies will tell you that this is obvious. They are born with a particular personality or temperamental style in place and start off life with it. But it doesn't mean they stay like that for ever. Early temperament is not by any means fixed and will change gradually over months and years according to their experiences and how they are handled. In other words, the personality of any developing child is a combination of what he was born with and what he has experienced subsequently.

It gets a little more complicated. Your baby's personality will affect how you handle him. A sunny, placid baby is easy to care for, stresses his parents less, and is therefore more likely to experience a sunny, placid mother. So: easy-going babies are easy to look after. They feed well and with pleasure, and they sleep soundly at predictable times. They enjoy novelty and stimulation without getting uncontrollably excited, and they can be jollied out of a crying spell. They like people and life in general. They produce a feeling of confidence and affection in those who care for them, so these babies themselves create a surrounding environment which is loving and luxurious. As they elicit good experiences for themselves, this helps them acquire feelings of security and confidence and their personality develops positively. They carry on being easy to live with.

In contrast, a baby who is hard to soothe is more likely to make any sleep-deprived mother impatient. Babies who are irritable, easily upset, frequently crying, intolerant of changes in their routine, apparently uncooperative and unpredictable are hard to live with. Such a temperament was called 'difficult' in a flash of inspiration by one group of developmental psychologists. They are certainly extremely difficult to look after. They make their care-givers lose confidence and they unwittingly surround themselves with irritability and unpredictability, as their mothers try a number of things in order to find something that will placate them. This is just the sort of situation they cannot tolerate, yet they are very likely to produce it by the effect they have on others around them. A vicious spiral develops. Their experience of this handling creates in them an apprehension of the world and a feeling of not being secure in it. They grumble, protest and despair openly, their parents become even more exasperated, handle them brusquely, they become more distressed and grumpy, and so the spiral continues.

Part of the reason babies like this are so difficult to care for is obvious. Irritable, quirky people who dislike changes in their lives demand more from others than cheerful people who are benign and unflappable. But there is another dimension. Parents tend to look to their children for an indication as to whether they are being good parents. If you have an easy baby who smiles at everything and is adaptable, you feel you are doing your job well. But if you have a gritty infant who protests about everything you do to him, you rapidly get the feeling that you are doing something wrong and maybe he doesn't even love you. It feels as though he's letting you know that you are an incompetent parent, and you begin to wonder whether you are coping at all. After all, you say to yourself, I should be able to have a smiling, satisfied child all the time, as I have given him such a perfect start.

Well, actually you can't. No one can. The mother who sets out to anticipate accurately her baby's every need and meet it without compromising principle, personal health or her relationship with her husband will produce an over-indulged, spoilt brat at the end of it. For babies, as for the rest of us, some frustration is necessary in order to stimulate us into developing new ways of coping and new insights (i.e. growing up). Some grit is necessary to produce a pearl (not that the oyster particularly enjoys the process).

In any case, judging your own parenting capacity by looking for short-term results in your child is doomed to failure. The personalities of babies and children are not just the result of parental handling. Babies are born with different temperamental styles and already have something on board at the start of things before any parent has got to them. They also have other experiences in life apart from those which parents provide. In any case, the amount of influence that parents have over their children's developing personalities is much less than most people (including quite a lot of professionals) think. Most parents provide entirely adequate parenting in the middle range of, for instance, the use of punishment or indulgence.

It is the extremes of parenting (repeated brutal punishment, serious neglect, unvarying indulgence, sexual abuse, continuing emotional blackmail and so on) which affect children's personalities, inevitably in a damaging way. For instance, all parents will criticise their child at some point; that is reasonable. But if that is *all* they do, *all* the time, that is extreme. The child gradually acquires a negative sense of himself, and reacts, depending on his own inherent temperament, by slowly sinking into depressed inertia or developing a defensive and aggressive style. Conversely, all parents should praise their offspring, but if they lavish unmitigated adoration on everything they do and indulge their child's every whim, then there will be hell to pay in the longer run when a small monster takes over the family. Even then, most children are remarkably proof against their parents' errors of judgement and have their own individual degree of resilience. Just think how different siblings are, one from another, in spite of having the same parents. Perhaps surprisingly, this is also true for non-identical twins, as their mothers will tell you. You simply cannot judge your capability as a parent just by looking at your child.

## LIVING WITH A DIFFICULT BABY

We need to make it clear that temperament is what is typical of a baby over a period of months – not something short-lived. Ill babies will (of course) be difficult while they are ill. A baby with reflux will be miserable because he is suffering, for instance. Babies can become jittery if over-tired and over-stimulated. (First babies are especially prone to over-stimulation; the three-week-old dressed in dungarees and baseball cap is probably being ambushed by more sensory input from all quarters than he can manage.)

Taking the longer view, however, you may have a baby who is typically grizzly, cries excessively when things go wrong, hates new things and is irregular in his biological rhythms (so that he doesn't sleep or get hungry at predictable times). This classic 'difficult' pattern, recognised by child development scientists, applies to about one baby in 15. Such a baby may smile infrequently, take hours to feed (perhaps without apparent pleasure), and then seem to be hungry less than two hours later. He will cry an enormous amount, yet it won't be possible to work out what he is protesting about. Whatever you do doesn't soothe him and if you try something new he hates it. You can never bank on getting a break because you don't know whether he's going to sleep for 10 minutes or an hour … and when he wakes up he will immediately start crying. What works one day doesn't work the next. It is a bit of a nightmare because you think you are supposed to be in control but don't feel that you are so your confidence plummets.

Older and more experienced mothers will say, 'She's got a difficult one there', just as they might say that about a difficult husband, 'I don't know how she puts up with him.' This is true wisdom, acknowledging as it does the role of the baby's inborn temperament. Unfortunately, the common assumption among many young(ish) adults is that your baby is in all respects a direct result of your parenting ability alone, that a baby's temperament or personality is completely the result of his upbringing. Although this has been shown to be wrong, it is still a common view. Friends and relatives may jump to the assumption that they could do better and are likely to offer unhelpful advice. It is infuriating and demoralising, but remind yourself that everyone believes himself or herself to be an expert when it comes to babies and child development!

Looking after a difficult baby is one of the most trying things anyone has to do. There are few inbuilt rewards in the short term and you have to run on good faith that what you are doing is the right thing. It is going to take a long time to work out what pattern of handling suits your baby. You need to trust your own sensitivity as to what he needs or likes without being drawn into impulsive chopping and changing. This can be tricky (to say the least), and to see it through you need support, not criticism disguised as advice. If only your friends were to say to you, as a more experienced parent might, 'You're so good with him', then you would feel more supported. They probably won't say anything like that, so you have to say it to yourself and make sure that your husband says it, too (and means it, having read all this). Mention to your friends that you have been told your baby has a difficult temperament and explain what that means.

Easy babies make it easy to be a 'good' parent; difficult babies make parents do all the work. And easy babies are more common than difficult ones, so not everyone has had the experience of knowing what the latter are like. One way of thinking about all this is to recognise that a difficult baby actually lacks certain attributes or skills which he hasn't developed so far (in spite of being perfectly intelligent):

- He doesn't yet have the capacity to soothe himself, which an easy baby demonstrates by the way he relaxes easily into sleep after a feed.
- He lacks the capacity to accept change and be fascinated by something new.
- He doesn't possess the self-regulation reflected in a steady rhythm of biological functions (sleep, hunger etc.).
- He can't seem to know when he is satisfied (so he over-feeds) or know what is required to make him satisfied (so he grumbles continually).

This means you have to do all this for him. He will develop these skills in time, but for the moment you have to fill in the gaps. He is, as it were, exporting his short-comings into you and you have to rise to the occasion in order to supply him with what he lacks by soothing him, reassuring him and adopting a steady, settled pattern of handling once you have sorted out, patiently and sensitively, what suits him as an individual. Imposing a rigid routine isn't likely to work, and if a certain routine seems to work for someone else's baby but not for yours, your confidence will be further undermined.

Because a difficult temperament is largely a reflection of things that have not yet developed (like self-soothing skills), it tends to ease in the longer run as these capacities mature. The most difficult baby, if treated with a reasonable (not perfect) degree of sympathetic and affec-tionate care from a parent who is quite clear that she is in charge, will eventually mellow. The personalities of most children change in their first few years. The risk is that parents lose their nerve and respond to a difficult, demanding baby by trying to gratify and indulge him at every turn. They then lose their self-confidence and feel powerless at the hands of an unappeasable tyrant.

The message is clear: if you have a relatively easy, sunny, tolerant baby, thank your lucky stars. He is making it easy for you to be a confident parent. If you have a difficult, unresponsive, demanding baby, you are being put on your mettle. You need to muster emotional support for yourself and carry on with what seems intuitively to you to be good-enough parenting (see page 235). Trust your own judgement and don't listen to his apparent criticism of how you are doing. Provide some degree of consistency and give him the affection he isn't very good at eliciting from you, rather than thrashing around in the hope that the magic answer will appear by accident. You have to supply him with what he lacks himself until he develops the skills for self-adaptation, self-regulation and self-soothing – which he will, so long as you can hang on in there. Ultimately things will improve.

# CHAPTER 17:

## Crying and inconsolable crying

Until about six weeks, when he starts to smile, a baby only has one method of direct communication, which is to cry. Before you have a baby of your own it seems as though it is going to be straightforward enough to deal with a crying baby – you find out what the cause is and sort it. But when you have your own baby it becomes more difficult: it is often far from clear why he is crying. Furthermore, the crying of your own baby is terribly stressful compared with the crying of someone else's, bad though that may be.

Indeed, there is no sound so upsetting and intrusive as your own baby crying, especially if there is no obvious reason. It is impossible to ignore and puts you in a series of unpleasant frames of mind: apprehensive, anxious, irritated, exasperated, feeling useless as a mother (or father), and sometimes downright bloody angry. Quite apart from your wish to ease your baby's distress, you experience a powerful feeling of being driven to stop it. This is something evolution has made a present of for you – it obviously helps the survival of the species if mothers are wired up to respond promptly to their offspring's distress. Evolution tends to have it in for mothers.

To a certain extent, babies have different types of cry for different types of discomfort. Experienced mothers who have got to know their babies well can often tell one sort of cry from another, sensing the difference between, for example, a hunger cry and a pain cry. However, they cannot do this on every occasion and certainly not to begin with, so every mother will have experienced the baby who cries persistently and she can't work out why.

**If a baby is crying, he is in distress or has a problem.** He will not cry 'to exercise his lungs', or for the hell of it, or just to get his own back on his mother, though it may sometimes feel like that. Nor, when tiny, will he cry in order to 'get his own way' (whatever that means). Don't listen to those who say, 'He's putting it on, there are no tears.' In the first few weeks of life crying babies don't produce tears. You will not spoil him by picking him up when he cries. Indeed, you may make him more secure. In one study, babies under one year old who were picked up soon after they started crying (not absolutely immediately after every whimper) cried less in their second year of life than those who had earlier been left to cry.

In order of likelihood, the most common causes of crying are:
- hunger
- tired yet unable to settle ('over-tired')
- discomfort: from wind, distension or being too hot or too cold
- pain: resulting from colic, reflux, ear infection, sore bottom or teething
- feeling ill and miserable – for example, because of a cold
- fright (short-lived and easily soothed)
- anger (also short-lived and usually obvious as to why).

Crying that persists, in spite of your best attempts to comfort your baby, needs active management. The timing of the crying may give you a clue as to what to do:

- Crying on and off during the day is likely to be caused by hunger or pain.
- Crying during a feed is likely to be caused by reflux. (See page 214.)
- Persistent crying only in the evenings falls into two categories, although these are probably extremes of the same problem:
  1. Evening fretting, which responds to straightforward measures such as picking him up, winding, trying a dummy or a feed, and pacing (see page 143).
  2. Colic – inconsolable crying which responds to none of the above (see page 146).

# HUNGER

The first thing to do with the problem of crying on and off throughout the day is to check your baby's weight gain. You may simply not have realised that his total daily intake of milk is insufficient because you are pleased that, when he is offered a feed, he seems to have a good appetite. A thriving baby who is eating well and putting on just under 450 g a fortnight is unlikely to be continually hungry. If he is underweight, then he is probably persistently hungry because his daily intake of milk is too low and the remedy is obvious: offer him longer at each feed, introduce an extra feed or two and, if you are breast-feeding, offer a top-up bottle at the end of a feed.

Two common causes for low nutritional intake are:

- A parent's (or maternity nurse's) premature enthusiasm for feeding routines with a breast-fed baby.
- Getting carried away with breast-feeding for its own sake without proper attention to the baby's weight gain. (Someone, even a healthcare professional, saying, 'It's fine, it's fine, there's no problem as long as you're breast-feeding.')

Very few babies have trouble absorbing enough nutrition from ordinary formula milks. Occasionally, though most unusually, your baby may be failing to gain weight because of some more complex problem. Discuss the matter with your health visitor or with your doctor.

# OVER-TIRED

Grandmothers frequently state that your baby is crying because he is 'over-tired'. You may think this is absurd because if the baby was tired he would go to sleep. Nevertheless, the sense of what they are saying is correct, although they are using an unhelpful word. Learning to fall asleep is a skill. What seems to happen is that some babies are slow to pick it up. Although they are tired, they lack the ability to fall asleep, especially if they have been hyped up. They cannot soothe themselves into a pre-sleep state, so cannot get started on the process of falling asleep. They do not know how to close their eyes and float; they have not yet found out how to suck their thumb and cannot, therefore, settle themselves to sleep.

This situation is worsened if they have just been stimulated and excited at the end of an already long and busy day. They feel uncomfortably tired but can do nothing to resolve it (and you, too, probably know the feeling). This makes them upset and irritable, so they find it even more difficult to relax and let go in order to fall asleep. Some of this is covered in the section on evening fretting (see page 143). Their obvious upset should elicit patient and soothing handling from their parents, but in practice this is not usually the case, especially if the parents are so tired themselves they would have no problem falling asleep in the middle of Piccadilly Circus.

Thumbs or fingers are good for comfort-sucking and therefore self-soothing for a baby who is tired or out-of-sorts. But when a baby is under 14 weeks old he can't reliably find his own thumb to suck, as he is too uncoordinated to get it into and keep it in his mouth. A dummy (see pages 91 and 186) is an excellent substitute, but your baby may have to learn how to use it. You will probably have to put it in his mouth and hold it in place for a few minutes to start with. A dummy offers the baby the chance to use sucking as a self-soothing activity.

If a small baby is not settling to sleep and cries when you put him down, try wrapping him up tightly by swaddling him (see page 91). This provides him with a sense of being contained and restrains his flailing limbs and his startle reflex. Some babies, like some adults, twitch as they are falling asleep. This is quite normal, but is a nuisance if it makes a baby's arms give such a violent jerk that it wakes him up. He will be startled into confused wakefulness and cry.

# WIND

One of the commonest assumptions is that crying is typically caused by wind. Certainly some babies swallow air during feeding and become uncomfortably distended. This is likely to be associated with crying a little time after a feed. They cry but this stops when their discomfort passes, quite literally, with a burp or fart. To wind your baby you don't have to hammer his back. Neither do you have to stand up. You might want to try sitting on an upright chair with your baby on your lap. Hold him with his back close to your tummy so that he is facing away from you. Pull him in so that he is right up against your stomach and then rock yourself, and him with you, slowly backwards and forwards.

Babies will root and try to suck when they are distressed in order to comfort themselves. Some mothers, noticing these attempts to suck, assume their baby is hungry and feed him. He then sucks for comfort but takes milk on board as well so gets uncomfortably distended. Discomfort makes him upset and he continues to suck for comfort, increasing his distension as he does so, and a vicious spiral is established. If your baby sucks only briefly when given a feed and then starts to cry, he is sucking for comfort in the face of distress such as distension – you should try a dummy (see page 91) – or he may have reflux (see below).

# GASTRO-OESOPHAGEAL REFLUX ('REFLUX')

This is a completely different problem from wind, and indeed colic – though it is often wrongly assumed to be the latter. It often goes undiagnosed. Essentially it is what it says it is: acid stomach contents refluxing up the oesophagus because the sphincter at the top of the stomach is too weak to prevent this happening. It produces a burning pain (heartburn) and understandably the baby cries. Unlike colic, it can happen during the day and at night, mainly during and after a feed. The baby will often have poor weight gain. It is truly distressing for baby and mother because it is evident that something is wrong.

Suspect reflux and consult your GP if any two of the following apply to your baby:

- He starts a feed eagerly but becomes distressed very soon after he starts to suck.
- Feeds take a long time because he breaks off and cries, sometimes going rigid and arching backwards.
- He has poor weight gain because he can only manage small amounts of milk at each feed.
- He becomes distressed if you lie him flat after a feed.
- He vomits after every feed.

Generally speaking, babies with reflux are miserable for most of the day. Their mothers are upset because they know that something is wrong, and are often further upset when healthcare professionals give superficial reassurance or suggest the mother may be depressed and ask her to complete a depression scale questionnaire.

Reflux responds well to medical treatments (Baby Gaviscon, for instance) coupled with giving your baby more frequent small feeds in an upright position and keeping him sitting up afterwards. If there is no improvement after a week or so, go back to your GP and ask to be referred to a paediatrician promptly. You may need to be quite assertive about this. If your baby has reflux, do not despair. Treatments work, and in any case it usually improves dramatically as the baby physically matures and when he starts on solid food.

## OTHER PAIN

A baby who has previously been relatively uncomplaining but then starts to cry throughout the day (and night) is possibly in pain because of an infection. A likely candidate is a middle ear infection for which he will need pain killers and perhaps antibiotics. This means taking him to the doctor to have his eardrums examined. If he has a middle ear infection he may well throw up, too, which can confuse you as to the source of the pain.

## COLIC (SERIOUS AND INCONSOLABLE CRYING)

Low grade, discontented grizzling in the evening between three and 12 weeks is typically because a windy baby cannot soothe and settle himself (see page 212). More determined evening crying, often accompanied by drawing his knees up, perhaps turning pale at the same time, will be colic. The management of colic is essentially the same as that of evening fretting but much more arduous.

No one knows what causes colic and no treatment has been shown to help all colicky babies. You can ask your doctor if there is any medicine that he would recommend for your baby. Simeticone (Dentinox, Infacol) drops, which prevent stomach contents foaming, or Gaviscon liquid, which forms a barrier against stomach acid, are often prescribed. Colief drops pre-digest lactose to diminish gassy fermentation of milk. The treatments can produce some improvement but usually not the total cure which you are hoping for. Dicycloverine (Merbentyl), which was often effective, is no longer recommended for babies under the age of six months because of a possible link with sudden collapse in a few cases.

There may not be a suitable or effective medicine for your baby, in which case the task for you is to survive until your baby grows out of it – by 14 weeks at the latest. Mark when this will be on a calendar and cross off each day that passes – that way it won't seem so endless. Until then you will have to comfort your baby each evening for several hours. The situation is truly ghastly. You may not be able to relieve his discomfort much, but his evening misery will do him no lasting harm physically or psychologically.

Do not blame yourself if your baby has colic. It does seem to run in some families but is not caused by any aspect of your diet or your state of mind. It helps enormously if you can share the burden of pacing up and down a room holding a screaming baby with another person. If your husband is unavailable, try to recruit some practical help from someone else. Do whatever seems best to you, which may include:

- Pacing with your baby over your arm, holding a dummy in position with your other hand (see 'tiger in a tree' hold on page 145: from three to six weeks old).
- Wheeling him up and down in the pram (inside or outside).
- Taking him for evening drives in the car.
- Rocking him in a cradle or bouncy chair (gentle rhythmic movements with a frequency of about two

rocks per second are often soothing though he may not actually fall asleep).
- Putting him in a papoose/baby sling to free your arms so at least you can get on with something else.

At about 11 weeks you may feel ready to crack. Grit your teeth and see it through. It is not your fault, your baby's nor your husband's and it will very soon be over.

# DON'T FEEL INADEQUATE

Not uncommonly, it is someone other than the parents who manages to settle a crying baby. Grandmothers can sometimes do this when his mother can't. They achieve it merely by sitting and rocking him for longer than the mother has had the patience or confidence to do. Mothers tend to be too anxious, tired or impatient to persist with soothing because they have other things to do and are worried that they are not doing the right thing anyway (or even 'letting him get away with it', spoiling him, etc.). It is always much easier if it isn't your baby. Get the issue of responsibility straight: your first duty is to survive – to be with your baby and try to comfort him. It is asking too much of yourself to remove the problem causing his unhappiness on every occasion. No parent, whatever the age of their child, has the responsibility to ensure their child's continual happiness. It just cannot be done.

A further reason for other people being able to settle your baby more easily than you can is because the baby may smell your milk. He may become distracted by this, even if he is not actually hungry, because the smell of milk reminds him of comfortable feelings, yet these are not what he is experiencing.

## TAKING A CRYING BABY INTO YOUR OWN BED

Although you may read warnings about taking your baby into your own bed, in practice nearly all parents have to, in desperation. There are obvious concerns about the danger of avoidable risks such as the baby overheating or being suffocated (see page 232) so don't put him under the duvet. You will also hear all sorts of tuttings and warnings to the effect that you are making a rod for your own back by setting up a bad habit. Quite frankly, after an hour's pacing, you will probably welcome a rod for your back; it would come in useful just to keep you upright. But there is a more serious point. More importantly, it means you (and he) can get some sleep that you would not otherwise have had. You will feel stronger the following day and have more opportunity to enjoy each other which is by far the more important issue.

## MEGA-STRESS

A baby who cries and cannot be soothed is a source of huge stress for any parent. You will sometimes feel exasperated, angry or desperate, and even furious with your baby. Such feelings are common and totally understandable. What is important is to recognise the signs of your own tension developing before you find yourself putting your baby down more roughly than you intended. If you ever feel about to lose your temper, immediately put your baby down gently in his crib or pram and walk into another room. Put some distance between the two of you so you can't lose your self-control and harm him. Shaking or squeezing a baby in anger is terribly, terribly dangerous.

It's a good idea to pick up the phone; it helps enormously to talk about your emotions with someone, preferably a friend who has herself had a crying baby, your mother or your husband.

There is a non-medical organisation called Cry-sis (www.cry-sis.org.uk) which has phone help lines manned by other, experienced volunteer parents until 10pm each evening. They are a practical source of support on desperate evenings. The telephone number is 08451 228 669 (08451 ACT NOW).

# CHAPTER 18:
## Depression

At about 10 weeks, you may well be feeling supremely exhausted and possibly demoralised, so how can you tell whether you have got depression? This is not rare in the weeks following childbirth – most studies suggest that, across the board, about one woman in 10 will experience some form of postnatal depression. It is probable that the sort of anticipatory planning and coping that we have talked about earlier in this book will minimise the likelihood of its occurrence, though it can't prevent every instance. If you have had depression before, then you are just a little more likely to experience it again at this stage, though this is certainly not inevitable.

Depression is more than feeling fed up or demoralised. It is a morbidly unhappy state that affects adversely all the positive things in one's mind: the capacity to enjoy; to look forward to events; to accommodate minor mishaps; to be realistic about one's shortcomings; to feel some self-confidence; and to summon up sufficient energy. If someone is depressed, they will usually experience irrational and unjustifiable guilt, anger and anxiety; will be tired but unable to sleep; cannot free themselves from pessimistic thoughts; and find themselves beset by painful doubts and memories.

Although the most obvious sign of depression following childbirth is bursting into tears frequently, some women may come across as irritable, or expressing worries that are hard for others to take seriously. Not all women who are depressed are predominantly tearful; they may be fighting it back. It is also the case that they will feel tired and lose their libido, but these particular symptoms are not very helpful indicators of depression in the first few months of new motherhood when fatigue and a lack of interest in sex are virtually universal.

## WHAT ARE THE KEY DANGER SIGNALS?

Firstly, there is an obvious change of mood, so that you find yourself bursting into tears repeatedly or snapping at your husband or mother in a way that just isn't you.

Secondly, and coupled with this, there are four typical patterns of thought and feelings, any of which are likely to be recognised by yourself or your husband. All these are exaggerations of occasional thoughts and feelings that are experienced by just about everyone:

- Serious loss of confidence, so that you feel persistently inadequate, incompetent and useless.
- Dreadful anxiety about your baby coupled with a sense of imminent disaster or a conviction that there is something horribly wrong with him that you haven't been told about.
- Persistently thinking that the baby is a mistake and that you have married the wrong guy. Everyone has such thoughts sometimes (particularly at about

eight weeks after childbirth) but in this instance you find you cannot rid yourself of them.

- Finding yourself getting repeatedly angry with your baby, even hating him, perhaps to the extent that you have to cover this up with an exaggerated public display of affection.

The third alarm bell is if you find you have stopped being able to get on with things. If you cannot manage to keep up with looking after your baby or your house/flat, consider whether it is just because you are exhausted or if it is more than that. Does everything feel like wading through treacle so that there is just too much to cope with? Does it seem as though a fog has descended and even the simplest thing, like taking the baby to be weighed, is a Herculean effort? Has getting out of the house become something you dread, and have you cancelled your last few social engagements? Are you finding that you are needing more and more help to get things done? If your ability to function is impaired beyond what you might expect from tiredness alone, then there may be a problem.

There is also a terribly rare but serious condition called puerperal psychosis, which may present with depressive features, although, more usually, it causes a confused excitement. If you develop this you are likely to hear voices which others can't hear, be muddled as to where you are and mistrust those around you. It needs urgent medical treatment; please don't assume it will get better on its own.

The difficulty is that women typically pretend to themselves that it's all right, that they aren't getting depressed because it would be shameful to admit to this. If they are breast-feeding they may be frightened they will be told to stop if they need medication. In any case it has become very hard for them to take any initiative to improve matters. At this stage, they need the support of someone to help them think clearly. Because depression ranges from severe to mild it is often necessary for another person to help you tell whether you have crossed the line between feeling extremely worn down and becoming depressed.

# TREATMENT

If you think any of the above applies to you, **the first thing to do is to talk about it** – with your husband, friend or health visitor. This is not easy because one of the perverse features of depression is a sense of failure and a belief that, in some way, it is your fault and you ought to be able to pull yourself together without outside help, even though this is patently impossible.

It has to be said that there is a risk of things going wrong at this point. Many husbands are also worried that you might be depressed and give impatient, superficial reassurance, or get in more help for you rather than tackling the fundamental issue. They may also be depressed themselves (depression in new fathers is not that rare), or fearful of stigma or the possibility of your being admitted to hospital. They may have an irrational concern that the only treatment option is for you to be prescribed what they think will be addictive, toxic antidepressants forever. There is also a risk that an inexperienced health visitor may do no more than administer a checklist called the 'Edinburgh Scale', tell you that your score indicates you are depressed, and offer to see you in two weeks(!). Pencil-and-paper checklists are occasionally still being used but are no longer recommended, because this sort of ineffectual practice can happen.

Sometimes putting everything into words is enough to reverse the depressive process, **but if not, you must consult your GP.** It is best if your husband goes with you because if you go alone you will almost certainly minimise your symptoms. Once again, the act of explaining how you feel to someone who is prepared to listen may prove sufficient help in its own right, especially if you come to realise that **becoming depressed at this time is in no way your fault and does not betray a previously unsuspected flaw in your personality.**

If talking about how you feel is not enough, there are more active treatments available.

It is increasingly recommended that cognitive therapy is the first treatment to be offered to a depressed woman with a baby. This involves you discussing your thoughts and the way in which you think with a therapist, often a psychologist or specially trained nurse (not normally the GP), who helps you to question some of your assumptions and beliefs. You are helped to change your thinking and thus your feelings in a positive direction. Although the treatment is effective it has to be said that therapists are in such short supply that this is not likely to be a realistic option.

It is not very likely that the sort of psychotherapy that concentrates on your own early relationships is going to be helpful at this stage.

There is no good evidence that light boxes or complementary medicine help, either.

Probably the most widely used treatment is antidepressant medication. This works, but only some antidepressant medicines are considered safe to use while breast-feeding (the ones that have such a tiny level present in breast milk they are considered to be of no risk to the baby), and the prescribing doctor needs to consider which of these is most appropriate. Be prepared for a discussion with your GP (again, preferably, your husband should be present) rather than accepting a dictum that all antidepressants are incompatible with breast-feeding.

This is where things can go wrong again. Some doctors and pharmacists go into zero-risk mode at this point, abdicate their professional responsibility to advise, and try to shift the decision about medication onto you. You have a right to choose whether or not to take antidepressants in the light of professional advice, of course. But by definition, if you are depressed and there is any hint of a risk to your baby, no matter how trivial, you will find it difficult to even think about your own needs.

The following medicines have such a low concentration in breast milk that the British National Formulary considers this too small to be harmful for babies, a point echoed by current NICE (National Institute for Health and Clinical Excellence) recommendations:

- sertraline (Lustral)
- lofepramine (Gamanil, Feprapax, Lomont)
- nortriptyline (Allegron)
- paroxetine (Seroxat).

Fluoxetine (Prozac), citalopram (Cipramil) and mood-stabilising drugs are **not** recommended when you are breast-feeding.

Antidepressants act to relieve depression and speed recovery; they are not tranquillisers (though some may make you drowsy). The important thing is to keep taking them for as long as you are advised to – don't stop as soon as you cheer up since you may find yourself slipping back down again. They often take a couple of weeks and sometimes a month to have the desired effect; don't expect an instant cure. Stick to the dose prescribed. You may need to take them for several months, but you needn't worry about getting addicted to them.

There isn't any evidence that 'natural' supplements or hormones such as progesterone help lift depression. St John's Wort might, but it is simply not known to be safe for breast-fed babies. (Indeed the data on its safety for adults, let alone for babies via breast milk, are minimal as it has not been through the standard assessments.)

Whichever approach is taken in your case, the general advice is to see it through. Not treating postnatal depression is not an option – it is horrible for you, and it can impair your baby's development and indeed, if it continues untreated, his relationship with you. It is absolutely no good simply hoping that it will clear up quickly on its own without professional attention. If you find yourself getting worse in spite of treatment then you must go back to your doctor. The problem is that partial treatment is likely to lead to a relapse. By definition you cannot snap out of depression using willpower alone – please don't believe the people who imply you can.

# CHAPTER 19:

## Medical matters

### IS MY BABY SERIOUSLY UNWELL?

If you are on your own during the day with an unhappy, grizzly baby, and you know he is not well, you will feel appallingly anxious as to what you should do. If, for instance, your baby is snuffling with a blocked-up nose and struggling with learning how to breathe through his mouth you will be understandably worried. You will find yourself checking and feeding him frequently. In such circumstances being a little 'overprotective' is perfectly healthy. You probably won't want to be labelled as neurotic, but if he seems to have more than just a cold how can you tell whether a professional should check him over?

**Firstly, if you are really worried about your baby, then your instincts are likely to be correct, as mothers usually know when their baby is not right.**

Otherwise, a doctor needs to see your baby if there are any of the following:

- breathing difficulties
- blood from anywhere

- a high temperature/fever
- vomiting 'everything'
- persistent watery diarrhoea
- a change in his cry
- he becomes limp and floppy
- he takes less than a third of his usual feeds ('drinks nothing')
- convulsions or anything you think might have been a fit.

## WORRYING ABOUT COT DEATH

It is normal to panic about the possibility of cot death. Yet it is important to get things into perspective as it is rare (the UK figure for the last year or two is about 1 in 2,500 babies). The term 'cot death' means a sudden, unexpected and unexplained death in a baby under a year old (usually under six months) while asleep. There has been considerable guesswork and controversy as to what causes this to happen. The most recent research suggests that the tiny number of babies who die unexpectedly have a subtle abnormality of the part of their brain that controls their breathing and temperature regulation. There is no way of knowing whether a baby has this abnormality beforehand. What might then transpire is that something happens while the baby is asleep which makes it more difficult for him to breathe freely, or overwhelms his ability to control his own temperature.

It is remarkably difficult to be balanced rather than alarmist when advising about the risk of cot death. Bear in mind that nothing you can do will completely prevent it happening; all you can do is reduce the risk. Nor does it mean that if you don't carry out official advice to the letter, your baby will die. This isn't an area in which there are guarantees one way or the other.

The only way of trying to identify what risk factors make cot death rather more likely is to collect information about babies who have died and compare their circumstances with those who have not. This is likely to point the finger at some factors that are not direct causes. There is no doubt that babies who sleep on their front or with bedding covering their face are more at risk; that is clear. On the other hand, it is far less clear to what extent sleeping in the same bed as the mother is a risk, since this depends on whether the mother smokes, how long the baby is in the bed, whether the baby is underneath a duvet and so on. Some aspects of sleeping together could be seen as protective. This means clear advice on the topic is difficult, and there is controversy among professionals as to what advice to give parents.

Any 'official' recommendations will inevitably play safe, whether the evidence is powerful (avoid tummy sleeping if possible) or inconsistent (as in not sleeping in the same bed). Lists of recommendations vary between countries and in any case change over time. Some individual professionals can be inappropriately messianic and rigid, striking fear into the hearts of parents by implying that any departure from official recommendations will inevitably be lethal.

You will have done as much as you can do to minimise the chances of cot death if you do the following:

- Put your baby to sleep on his back. This is a crucial recommendation. Cot deaths have been halved since this has been usual practice.
- Make sure you and he don't fall asleep together on the sofa or in a chair.

- Don't let him sleep all night in your bed if you are a smoker or have been drinking alcohol.
- Don't let him overheat. Avoid:
  - putting his cot/crib too close to a radiator in winter or allowing the bedroom to get too hot (no more than 20°C)
  - wrapping him up in too many clothes or blankets – he should never sweat
  - letting him sleep with a hat on, as his head needs to be exposed in order for him to lose heat.
- Place him with his feet near the bottom of the crib or cot (so he can't wriggle down beneath the blanket).
- Don't let anyone smoke in the room the baby sleeps in.
- Have him sleep in the same room as yourself in a separate basket, crib or cot for the first six months (see Chapter 4).
- Call a doctor if your baby is unwell.

There is no evidence that swaddling your baby increases the risk of cot death. Immunisations and using a dummy to settle a baby both reduce the risk.

Try not to worry too much about this tragedy happening to you. All of us would give anything to be able to wave a magic wand over our offspring and ensure they never have an accident or illness and live happily until they are 90. This just can't be done.

# ACCIDENTS

Like cot deaths, you can't absolutely ensure these won't happen. Nevertheless, there are several avoidable causes of accidents in the first six months:

- Someone drops the baby or he falls off a surface.
  - Let older children know that they must not pick up the baby if there is no adult present.
  - Do not put bouncing cradles on tables or work-surfaces, as bouncing causes them to move.
  - Never turn your back or leave your baby unattended on a changing trolley – he can roll off, **even if you know he can't**. If the doorbell rings, take him with you.
- The baby chokes on a small object. Babies who have learned to pick objects up will transfer them to their mouths. Keep a wary eye on what your baby can reach and prohibit other children from giving him sweets or peanuts.
- Burns from over-hot bathwater, a kettle on a worktop which is pulled over or a drink which has been heated unevenly in a microwave and has hot spots, even though the few drops you test don't seem to be too hot.
- Drowning, especially if left momentarily in the bath. (Once again, wrap him in a towel and take him with you to answer the door.)
- Overheating in a parked car in sunlight, or being too close to a radiator.

**Always take a baby to hospital if he:**
- has fallen, hit his head and been knocked unconscious
- has swallowed something dubious (if you know what it is, berries or pills, for example – take a sample with you to the hospital)
- has been burned (while in transit, keep the affected part cold by immersing it in water and ice)
- has breathing difficulties
- seems to have had a fit.

# CHAPTER 20:
## Some principles of 'good-enough' parenting

Although you are now a parent, you are not necessarily a confident expert on babies and childcare. You will receive a ton of advice, much of it delivered in certainties such as 'You must ...' or 'Never ...' or 'They always ...' Some findings from the systematic study of child development are surprising and overturn what would appear to be received wisdom or the assumptions that many people make. Before you take too much advice on board, here are some broad principles of parenting in the light of what is known about child and parent development:

1. *The first duty of a parent is to survive*
The most important responsibility towards your baby is to be available, not to rear the perfect child (thank goodness). This doesn't mean that you have to remain physically close to your baby all the time, rather that you should be a constant and generally available figure throughout childhood.

2. *Parents are perfect if they are 'good enough'*
They don't have to get everything right; luckily, babies are, by and large, parent-proof. You can make mistakes and it won't matter much. In any case, the influence that ordinary parents have on the development of their children is rather less than most non-professionals think. This is just as well, as most parents cannot be entirely in control of their own lives, let alone remain utterly consistent and wonderful. If parents can keep their child and his best interests in mind, remain sensitive to his experience of the world and respond appropriately to his needs as a separate person, they are doing more than enough.

3. *It's not what you do, it's the way that you do it*
Attitudes and relationships count for more than procedures and practices. For instance, from the point of view of your baby's personality development, it doesn't matter at all in the long term whether you breast-feed or bottle-feed. As a rough rule of thumb, parents who can provide love for the child as he is, coupled with a measure of respect for him as a separate person, are going to do the right thing in terms of handling the child. Exactly what they do is less important than establishing a loving relationship between themselves and their child.

4. *Accept and enjoy your child for who he is ...*
... not who you think he should be or who you want him to become. Babies and children are not just empty vessels into which you pour instructions, affection and information. They play an active part in their own development and won't end up just like you or how you would like them to be.

### 5. *Do as you would be done by*

By and large, if you do what seems to you to feel right and reasonably safe, and do for your baby what you would have liked to have done to you when you were a baby, then you are unlikely to go seriously wrong. Be faithful to your own intuition, it's what it is there for.

### 6. *You can't judge your worth as a parent just by the development or behaviour of your baby*

Babies are individuals from day one and some aspects of development are beyond the influence of parents. Gender is one, of course, but the baby's early temperament is another. Babies' behaviour and development don't necessarily provide parents with immediate feedback as to whether they are doing the right thing! Often you have to do what you instinctively think is right, even if it doesn't have an immediate effect on your child in the way you want. Do not be afraid of your own experience, judgement and authority. In all of these respects you are ahead of your child and you should stay in charge. Stick to your guns and don't just look to your child to reassure you that you are doing the right thing.

### 7. *Look after yourself and your marriage/relationship as well as your baby*

Babies and children are only passing through your life. They are on loan to you. If you sacrifice yourself completely to their needs so that you have no time for your husband, you may lose him and therefore rob the child of his father. In a similar vein, if you are, by the time your baby is a young adult, a mother and nothing else, your offspring's departure from your side and entry into the wider world will take from you all that you are. He may feel too guilty about this to abandon you. You will not have reared an independent person. Parents who live vicariously through their children run the risk of producing children who feel they have to satisfy their parents rather than live their own lives.

8. *Don't get hung up on having to get it all perfect right from the start*
Continuing processes count for more than beginnings. We don't think perfect starts are that important and no one has sufficient control over the process to achieve one in any case. We have simply tried to tell you how to make it more likely that all three of you get off to a *good-enough* start – which is what really matters.

# Afterword: Coda

At some point it will dawn upon you that you have come through. Life without your baby seems unimaginable; it is as if he has always been there. You have another loving relationship in your life and you now have a real family. In the last few months you will have learned things about your baby, yourself and your husband, and you have become more complex, mature and wise. Colic and patchy nights permitting, you will also be a more fulfilled individual, too. You have become an established parent as well as all the other things you are. From now on your confidence in your new responsibilities will grow and your energies will return. This is the time for you to enjoy your baby, and to enjoy yourself.

# Index

# INDEX